The Mexican Cult of Death
in Myth and Literature

D1027616

University of Florida Monographs
Humanities, No. 44

The Mexican Cult of Death in Myth and Literature

Barbara L. C. Brodman

A University of Florida Book

The University Presses of Florida
Gainesville · 1976

EDITORIAL COMMITTEE

Humanities Monographs

Library of Congress Cataloging in Publication Data

Brodman, Barbara, 1943–
    The Mexican cult of death in myth and literature.

    (University of Florida monographs: Humanities;
no. 44)
    "A University of Florida book."
    Bibliography: p.
    1.   Short stories, Mexican—History and criticism.
2.   Mexican fiction—20th century—History and criticism.
3.   Death in literature. I. Title. II. Series:
Florida. University, Gainesville. University of
Florida monographs: Humanities; no. 44.
PQ7207.D4B7   863'.01   76-26105
ISBN 0-8130-0556-6

TYPOGRAPHY BY THE STORTER PRINTING COMPANY
GAINESVILLE, FLORIDA

PRINTED BY BOYD BROTHERS INCORPORATED
PANAMA CITY, FLORIDA

Preface

Para el habitante de Nueva York, París o Londres, la muerte
es la palabra que jamás se pronuncia porque quema los
labios. El mexicano, en cambio, la frecuenta, la burla, la aca-
ricia, duerme con ella, la festeja, es uno de sus juguetes fa-
voritos y su amor más permanente. Cierto, en su actitud hay
quizá tanto miedo como en la de los otros; mas al menos no
se esconde; la contempla cara a cara. . . . El desprecio a la
muerte no está teñido con el culto que le profesamos.[1]

THUS OCTAVIO PAZ describes a cultural phenomenon
which has for centuries fascinated scholars and *aficio-
nados* of virtually every field of Mexican studies—"el culto a la
muerte," the cult of death, a term which readily calls to the mind
of anyone familiar with Mexico and her culture the unusually
constant place of death in the minds and lives of the Mexican people. Death is, so to speak, a constant companion of the Mexican
in his journey through life.

The purpose of this study is twofold. It is primarily to discuss
the literary manifestations of the Mexican cult of death, a topic
which, because of its vastness, I have chosen to limit to the spe-
cific discussion of its occurrences in the contemporary Mexican
short story. Representative authors and works are Juan Rulfo, *El
llano en llamas*; José Revueltas, *Dormir en tierra*; Rosario Castellanos, *Ciudad Real*; Carlos Fuentes, *Los días enmascarados*;
Guadalupe Dueñas, *Tiene la noche un árbol*; and Eraclio Zepeda,
Benzulul.

The fame of the first four of these authors rests heavily upon
the novel. I have chosen, though, to discuss the manifestations of
the cult of death in their short stories. My reasons for doing so

1. Octavio Paz, *El laberinto de la soledad* (Mexico 1965), p. 48.

are the following: First, I feel that the short story, dealing as it does generally with one theme or aspect of the world it depicts, is the ideal literary form in which to seek manifestations of an isolated phenomenon such as the cult of death. Second, I feel that as a genre the short story has suffered unfair and frequent critical neglect, and I agree with José López Valdizón when he says, "no hay género literario fácil y el cuento está considerado entre los más difíciles. Esto por su extensión, su dinámica y la síntesis que presuponen tales condiciones. . . . el cuento es esencia y obedece a una estructura propia e intransferible."[2] And, third, I have found that in regard to manifestations of the cult of death, little, if anything, would be gained by discussing them in relation to the novel rather than the short story, for manifestations of the cult of death in the novels of these authors, though slightly more embellished, are generally highly consistent with those found in their short stories.

The second purpose of this study is to discuss the historical bases of the phenomenon, for the cult of death in Mexico is not merely a literary phenomenon, nor is it a recent one. It is, rather, a social phenomenon whose roots are buried deep in the soil formed by the union of two distinct cultures, each of which possessed a perceptible cult of death and each of which imparted certain aspects of that cult to the culture of which it was cocreator. I therefore feel that a necessary preliminary to any discussion of the manifestations of this phenomenon in its contemporary state must be a discussion of the historical bases upon which it was founded, and since we are concerned primarily with the literary manifestations of the phenomenon, a discussion of its literary bases is also in order.

It should be noted, though, that the purpose of this book is not to study literary influences, but rather to establish the existence of a state of mind and to use as proof its sustained reiteration as a literary theme in pre-Conquest and contemporary literature. Literary references in the first three chapters of this study are therefore not to be interpreted as having directly influenced the later works discussed in Chapter Four. They are provided, rather, as an aid to acquiring a more concrete background for the understanding of the term "cult of death."

2. José López Valdizón, "Tres aspectos técnicos del cuento," *Comunidad* 3(14):369.

Before beginning the discussion of the manifestations of the cult of death in the contemporary Mexican short story, I shall therefore discuss the historical and literary bases of the phenomenon, relating them to the two pre-Conquest cultures from which modern Mexican culture generates; and I shall examine the present-day sociological and psychological implications of the cult, showing it to constitute an integral part of the psyche of the present-day Mexican, thereby logically manifesting itself in contemporary Mexican literature.

In this manner I hope to provide a far more comprehensive and defined picture of the cult of death and its relationship to literature in Mexico than has heretofore been provided by social scientists or literary scholars. One finds that the Mexican cult of death as a social phenomenon has been discussed and alluded to by numerous scholars in that field. No one, however, has attempted to combine in one study the observations and findings of all of these to provide a succinct, comprehensive analysis of the origins and nature of the phenomenon and its relationship to contemporary literature. This I propose to do.

to my parents,
ELENORE and WAYLAND CAMPBELL,
for all they are and do

Contents

1. Historical and Literary Bases of the   1
   Cult of Death in Mexico

2. Historical and Literary Bases of the   19
   Cult of Death in Spain

3. The Cult of Death as a Social Phenomenon   37

4. Manifestations of the Cult of Death in the   47
   Contemporary Mexican Short Story

5. Literary Influences Today: New Trends   83
   in Mexican Literature

References   87

Para los antiguos mexicanos la oposición entre muerte y vida no era tan absoluta como para nosotros. . . . Vida. muerte y resurrección eran estadios de un proceso cósmico, que se repetía insaciable. La vida no tenía función más alta que desembocar en la muerte, su contrario y complemento; y la muerte, a su vez, no era un fin en sí; el hombre alimentaba con su muerte la voracidad de la vida, siempre insatisfecha.

Octavio Paz

A Ayocuan

Entretéjanse flores azules y flores color de fuego:
tu corazón y tu palabra, oh príncipe chichimeca Ayocuan.
Por un breve instante hazlas tuyas aquí en la tierra.

Lloro porque nuestra muerte las destruye,
ay, destruya nuestras obras: los bellos cantares,
por un breve instante házlos tuyos en la tierra.

Anonymous

1

Historical and Literary Bases of the Cult of Death in Mexico

T O UNDERSTAND THE BASES of the Mexican cult of death, one must look back first to the basic religious beliefs of pre-Conquest Mexico, for every phase of life throughout the development of Mexican culture was integrally bound with religion. According to that religion, the world in which the pre-Conquest Mexican lived was the fifth world, or Sun, to have been created, the other four having been destroyed one by one before the fifth world came into being. That world was to meet the same fate as its predecessors, the means of destruction this time, as determined by the birth sign *naui ollin*, being a series of cataclysms culminating in the release of "monsters of the twilight who await the fatal hour beneath the western sky, [and] will swarm out and hurl themselves upon the last survivors" [1:96].

It was a world which had been created through the blood and sacrifice of the gods. The story of that creation, as it was told by native informers to Fray Bernardino de Sahagún shortly after the Conquest, is as follows:

> 4. —Decían que antes que hubiese día en el mundo que se juntaron los dioses en aquel lugar que se llama *Teotihuacan*, . . . dijeron los unos a los otros dioses: "¿Quién tendrá cargo de alumbrar al mundo?"
>
> 5. —Luego a estas palabras respondió un dios que se llamaba *Tecuciztécatl*, y dijo: "Yo tomo cargo de alumbrar al mundo." Luego otra vez hablaron los dioses, y dijeron: "¿Quién será otro?"
>
> 7. —Uno de los lios [sic] de que no se hacía cuenta y era buboso, no hablaba sino oía lo que los otros dioses decían, y los otros habláronle y dijéronle: "Sé tú el que alumbres, bubosito." Y él de buena voluntad obedeció a lo que le mandaron y respondió: "En merced recibo lo que me habéis mandado, sea así."

12. —Después que se acabaron las cuatro noches de su penitencia, . . .

13. —. . . ardió el fuego cuatro dias.

14. —. . . y luego los dos sobredichos se pusieron delante del fuego, . . .

16. —[Tecuciztécatl] cuatro veces probó, pero nunca se osó echar. . . .

17. —. . . los dioses luego hablaron a *Nanautzin* y dijeron: "¡Ea pues, Nanauatzin, prueba tú!"

18. —Y como le hubieron hablado los dioses, esforzóse y cerrando los ojos arremetió y echóse en el fuego, . . . y como vió Tecuciztécatl que se habia echado en el fuego, y ardía, arremetió y echóse en el fuego.

21. —Después que ambos se hubieron arrojado en el fuego, y después que se hubieron quemado . . .

23. —. . . los dioses se hincaron de rodillas para esperar a dónde saldría Nanauatzin hecho sol. . . .

25. —. . . primero salió el sol y tras él salió la luna; por el orden que entraron en el fuego por el mismo salieron hechos sol y luna.

26. —. . . tenían igual luz con que alumbraban. . . .

27. —. . . Y luego uno de los dioses fué corriendo y dió con un conejo en la cara a Tecuciztécatl, y oscurecióle la cara y ofuscóle el resplandor, y quedó como ahora está su cara.

28. —Después que hubieron salido ambos sobre la tierra estuvieron quedos, sin moverse de un lugar el sol y la luna; y los dioses otra vez se hablaron, y dijeron: "¿Cómo podemos vivir? ¿No se menea el sol? ¿Hemos de vivir entre los villanos? Muramos todos y hagámosle que resucite por nuestra muerte."

29. —Y luego el Aire se encargó de matar a todos los dioses y matólos. . . .

31. —. . . y después que el sol comenzó a caminar la luna se estuvo queda en el lugar donde estaba.

32. —. . . de esta manera se desviaron el uno del otro y así salen en diversos tiempos. . . .   [2:I,258–61]

In this theory of creation through sacrifice lay the latent seed from which would spring, years later, the bloody religious ritual of the Aztecs, based on the rationalization that "if only the death of the gods could make possible the movement and life of the Sun, then only the sacrifice of men, who play the role of the gods

on earth, can maintain its life and motion" [3:31]. Only through
self-sacrifice could man postpone the cataclysms which were destined to put an end to the Sun and preserve it from the same destiny of its predecessors.

Thus, the earth was born of death and doomed to catas-
trophe⌞And the Mexican,* by his very concept of creation, was
deprived of any control over his life or destiny.⌡His was a fatalistic
concept of life, every phase of which was ruled by determinism
and overshadowed by the omnipresent specter of death. Thus, in
his book on Mexican art, Justino Fernández speaks of the first
Mexican temples as "proof of an ancient but already well-
developed culture, with evidence of a cult of the dead" and points
out that "the image of death appears in Mexican art in one way
or another from the earliest period to the present time" [4:9, 13].
Or, in the words of Jacques Soustelle, "Death and life are no more
than two sides of the same reality; from the earliest times the
potters of Tlatilco made a double face, one half alive and the
other skull-like, and the dualism is also to be found in innumerable documents. Perhaps no people in history have been so much
haunted by the grim presence of death as the Mexicans, but for
them life came out of death as the young plant comes from the
mouldering seed of the earth" [1:106].

As time went on these basic myths were embellished and ex-
panded upon to form various religious sects. The most important
of these prior to the appearance of the Aztecs as an organized tribe
(ca. A.D. 1200) was that based upon the person and doctrine of
Quetzalcóatl. This god-king was the inspiration for one of the
world's truly beautiful religious myths, and his doctrine added a
new dimension to Mexican religious philosophy and to the cult
of death.

*A brief explanation of terms may be in order at this time. The term "Aztec"
refers to the language and people of Tenochtitlan. It is the term adopted by the
Spaniards based upon the mythological place from which the Aztecs believed
they came, Lake Aztlán. Most students of language refer to the immediate group
of Uto-Aztecan languages, of which Aztec was one, as Nahuatl. Classical Nahuatl
is a "dead" literary language based upon the language of Tenochtitlan and re-
duced to writing shortly after the Conquest by the Franciscan missionaries. It is
from this language that the works cited herein have been translated. I use the term
"Nahuatl" to refer not only to the language, but also to the peoples and cultures
who used this language prior to the Conquest, exclusive, that is, of the Aztecs, to
whom I refer as such. I have also used the more general term "Mexican" inter-
changeably with all of the above. This I find is a tendency common among modern
Mexicans.

Quetzalcóatl appears to have been ruler, for approximately twenty years, of the Toltec city of Tula, built between A.D. 900–1156. He was conceived when his mother swallowed a stone of jade, a symbolic representation of the soul of man, suggesting his heavenly, spiritual origin. As a ruler he postulated a doctrine based upon prayer and penitence. Despite some wizards and sorcerers who encouraged him to accept human sacrifice, Quetzalcóatl was opposed to such practices, preaching instead the sacrifice of snakes and butterflies. High dignitaries, according to his doctrine, should be "virtuous, humble and peace-loving, considerate and prudent, not frivolous, but grave and austere and jealous of custom, loving, merciful, compassionate and a friend to all, and devout and fearful of god . . ." [5:27]. Knighthood was achieved through contemplation, humiliation, and detachment, the ceremony consisting of forty to seventy days of fasting and contemplation in a locked temple, subjection to taunts, insults, physical attacks, and filthy conditions, culminating in a visit to the Great Temple where the initiates received the doctrine by which they would live their lives. "The central part of these Tests of Initiation is the detachment taught by Quetzalcóatl as a means of liberation from duality" [5:68]; that is, the liberation of the spirit from the body, an obvious exaltation of the spiritual life. "It is significant that the demons who decide, because of Quetzalcóatl's irritating purity, to cause his downfall invent exactly the trick of 'giving him his body' " [5:56].

This the wizard Tezcatlipoca does first by showing to Quetzalcóatl his reflection in a mirror, then by tricking him into getting drunk and sleeping with a woman thereby breaking his vow of celibacy. Having committed these grave errors, Quetzalcóatl decides to leave his people and travel east to the shores of the "divine water," the gulf coast. There he sets himself on fire and burns to death. He descends into the region of the dead where he gathers up the bones of a dead man and woman and brings them to life with his own blood. On the eighth day he rises to the heavens to become the great star Venus called, by the Mexicans, "Quetzalcóatl." "The spiritual content of the Quetzalcóatl myth is self-evident. The anguish for his sin, his burning need for purification, and, also, the fire that converts him into light reveal a religious doctrine closely related to those humanity has known elsewhere under various symbolic languages" [5:54].

The blood of Quetzalcóatl, the "divine fire," symbolizes the blood of the Redeemer who, through his own sacrifice, brings about man's birth into spirituality. The soul follows the same symbolic route taken by Quetzalcóatl. "She descends from her celestial home and enters the darkness of matter only to rise again, glorious, at the moment of the body's dissolution. The myth of Quetzalcóatl signifies just this. The King's absolute purity refers to the state of the planet when it is still nothing but light. His sins and remorse correspond to the phenomenon of the incarnation of this light and the painful, but necessary, assumption of human form; his abandonment of the things of this world and the fatal fire he builds with his own hands show the precepts which have to be followed if human existence is not to be lost, the attainment of eternal unity through detachment from and sacrifice of the transitory self" [5:59]. Thus, with Quetzalcóatl the concepts of death and sacrifice suffer no loss of importance as basic religious concepts, but take on a more symbolic significance.

We see, then, that death and sacrifice were outstanding elements of the religious myths of the Mexican peoples, indicating that from the beginning death was accorded a position of extreme importance in their culture. Everything had been created through the death of the gods, and with destruction it was wholly bound. With Quetzalcóatl and the religious doctrine which grew up around him, the profoundly deterministic nature of Mexican religious philosophy was tempered to allow for the possibility of man's being able to achieve some sort of spiritual state which would allow him to detach himself from his finite world. It was with this particular doctrine that the Mexicans came closest to exhibiting any real kinship to the religious doctrine of their future conquerors. But long before any contact between these cultures could take place, the doctrine of Quetzalcóatl had been corrupted and replaced by a new doctrine.

With the Aztecs and the advent of the Era of Huitzilopochtli, the doctrine of Quetzalcóatl lost much of its symbolic significance. "The idea of feeding the sun with a symbolic heart, created within man's psyche, was very soon distorted. Offerings to the gods made in flowers picked from the meadows and cornfields became offerings of enemy hearts torn out" [5:75]. "The laws of interior preparation revealed by Quetzalcóatl were used by the Aztecs to prop up their bloody state. The mystic union with the divinity, which the individual could achieve only by successive steps and after a life of contemplation and penitence, was thenceforth considered to be the result merely of the manner of a man's death. We are here dealing with low witchcraft, the material transmission of human energy to the sun" [5:28].

A thorough discussion of the reasons behind the Aztecs' development of their bloody, death-oriented religious rites would be far too long and superfluous to the main topic of this study to be attempted here, but it is worthwhile to note that the *guerras floridas,* waged with the primary purpose of acquiring sacrificial victims, and the sacrificial rites themselves, were by no means purely religious manifestations, but also extremely powerful and effective political tools. Thus, a death cult such as we see in Mexico today is but a logical outgrowth of a culture which was once one of the most death-oriented in the world.

Much of Aztec thought may be attributed to the teachings of the powerfully influential priest-politician Tlacaélel. It was he who persuaded the Aztecs that their god was Huitzilopochtli, the Sun, and that by providing him with enough of the vital energy contained in the blood and hearts of their own kind, they could postpone indefinitely the destruction of the fifth Sun. Therefore, instead of a religion oriented more toward spiritual concerns based on an absolute assurance of the world's impending physical destruction, a religion sprang up in which the primary concern was for the maintenance of the physical state of the world and which was devoid of any concern for the individual.

> According to Aztec religion . . . man has no other aim on earth but to feed the Sun with his own blood, without which the Sun will die of exhaustion. This tragic dilemma obliges him to choose between indulging in massacre or bringing about the end of the world. So each victim, aware of his cosmic mission, cheerfully allowed his heart to be torn out, and . . . the Aztec chroniclers preserved the names of certain warriors whose specially heroic deaths were held up for emulation. But, if we do not passively accept these official declarations, if we refuse to regard it as natural that customs should be perpetuated which, whatever their time and place, are monstrous, we may begin to perceive that we are here dealing with a totalitarian state of which the philosophy included an utter contempt for the individual. . . . According

to the testimony of all the chroniclers, Spanish and native alike, it appears on the surface that any freedom of thought or action was inconceivable in the Aztec world.   [5:14]

Certainly many sacrificial victims willingly, with great pride, mounted the temple steps to have their hearts torn out, considering themselves saviors of the world and reincarnations of the gods who had performed a similar act to create life. Also, since the Aztecs believed that it was the manner of a man's death and not his conduct in life which determined his spiritual destiny, death in battle or on the sacrificial stone was often pursued as it carried with it the reward of attaining one of the most desirable of the several Aztec heavens.

The stories of ritual sacrifices in which the victim went with willingness to meet his fate are many in both native and Spanish chronicles. They reflect the extent to which the bloody doctrine of the Aztecs had permeated the minds and everyday lives of the people who lived under its sway.

Every month, and there were eighteen in the Aztec solar calendar, had its ceremonies and festivals with the usual sacrifices. Sometimes sacrificial victims were destined by birth to represent a particular god on the sacrificial stone; sometimes the victims were prisoners of war; sometimes they were women, and, sometimes, children. Most were laid across the convex sacrificial stone, arms and legs held down by four priests while the fifth slashed the breast with an obsidian knife, pulled out the still-beating heart, and burnt it as an offering to the god. The body was then rolled down the temple steps where it was prepared by other priests for a cannibalistic communion rite, often partaken of by the entire population.

Other sacrificial rites were those to the fire god, Huehueteotl, in which victims were first thrown into a fire and then fished out still alive to have their living hearts torn out and offered to the god, or those in the last month of the year, in which victims were tied to a stake and killed with arrows. It was also permissible and common practice for wealthy merchants and dignitaries to buy slaves in the market place to be used as sacrificial victims and served to guests in their homes. In some months there were weeks of ceremonies and parades in which the priests danced in the flayed skins of sacrificial victims. Any one of these spectacles, to us so abominable, was a common and accepted occurrence to the pre-Conquest Mexican.

This may help to explain how, in the fifth month of every year, a young prisoner of war, fattened and treated as a god for one year, went proudly and stoically to his death, sincerely believing himself to be the incarnation of the god Tezcatlipoca, or how a famous captured Tlaxcallan general, Tlalhuicoltzin, having refused the freedom and honors offered to him by Moctezuma II by virtue of his gallant past record, should accept the command of Moctezuma's armies in a war against the Tarascans, defeat them completely, return loaded with booty and prisoners, and still refuse his freedom, begging for and receiving instead "the honorable death of a soldier on the sacrificial stone of Him who had vanquished him, the 'teotl' Huitzilopochtli" [7:117].

These are only a very few of the many examples of Mexicans who had been indoctrinated sufficiently in their bloody religion to be able to accept and support the ritual of human sacrifice, even when the sacrifice was their own. But it is evident that many looked upon these rites with fear and horror and saw them as mere tools of political oppression. The guerras floridas, waged, in theory, for the purely religious purpose of securing sacrificial victims, were in reality "concebidas con un interés político. . . . Si se piensa que durante los cuarenta años de su formación el Estado azteca ha vivido sobre la ley de la fuerza, nos persuadimos que la santificación de la violencia era la única salida lógica nada más eficaz para dominar una población, en gran parte constituida por hordas mercenarias y por sobrevivientes de ciudades devastadas, que el terror sagrado que se instala entonces sobre la metrópoli" [8:147].

" 'We do not believe,' said the Aztecs, 'we fear' " [9:116]. And how else could one explain the existence of written rules concerning procedures in the event of unwillingness to be sacrificed or penalties—of death, of course—to be imposed upon anyone refusing to witness a sacrifice? Or, why else would cities such as Tlaxcala and Texcoco, with the same religious tradition as the Aztecs, so readily ally themselves with the Spaniards against Moctezuma? "This hostility towards the Aztecs seems to show that the belief in a holy war which the latter so freely propagated has been taken more seriously by modern students than by the Mesoamerican peoples themselves. If faith in the general cosmic need for ritual killing had existed, these betrayals would have been unthinkable, the more so since, as archaeology has proven, the Nahuatl religion was firmly rooted throughout Mexico" [5:44].

It appears, then, that Aztec religion was a corruption of traditional Nahuatl religion and that it was almost entirely the result of political necessity. But whether the people feared or believed in this religion, the fact still remains that such an extremely death-oriented religion did exist and that it created the situation whereby, regardless of whether they feared it or believed in it, death was a constant in the life of every Mexican during the Aztec era.

It is most difficult for the European or North American to truly understand the Mexican concept of death and its relationship to life. We, who are so extraordinarily afraid of death, though we have created numerous interpretations of the phenomenon, have always seen it as something opposed to life, in contradistinction to it. The Mexican, on the other hand, from his most primitive myth of creation, saw life as indivisibly united to death. Together these two states of being created the whole of the natural order of things. One without the other would have been incomplete and inconceivable, and, therefore, one was not preferable to the other. This explains the frequent representation of the dual aspect of life in Mexican art—the living aspect of one side of a sculpture and the skeletal aspect of the other—and the realistic representations of death so often reflected there.

Since an awareness of death permeated every aspect of the life of the ancient Mexican, it is understandable that it provided the motive for some of his finest art. In literature, death was an outstanding motif. Since "to die . . . was to accomplish an act of incalculably far-reaching potentialities" [9:115], it was quite logically a major preoccupation of the great ancient Nahuatl poet-philosophers. Let us examine, therefore, some representative examples of pre-Conquest Nahuatl literature and see how they reflect the authors' artistic preoccupation with death.

I have chosen to restrict the discussion of pre-Conquest Nahuatl literature to the field of lyric poetry. This I do not only for the sake of brevity, but also because I feel that lyric poetry was the best vehicle for personal expression in pre-Conquest Mexico, and it is with the establishment of the existence of a cult of death

in the minds of the people of the culture, and its subsequent manifestation in their literature, that I am most concerned. That death
was an outstanding theme in other forms of poetry, epic and dramatic, and in the prose of the period also is certain, but these
genres, being vehicles more of religious and political expression,
represent what might be called the causal rather than the effectual
genres of pre-Conquest Nahuatl literature as they relate to the cult
of death.

Angel María Garibay, one of the world's foremost authorities
on ancient Nahuatl literature, divides lyric poetry into five categories. The first of these contains essentially three types of lyric
poems, Cuauhcuicatl, Teuccuicatl, and Yaocuicatl (*canto de
águilas, canto de príncipes,* and *canto de guerra*), which celebrate
"la santidad de la guerra, la dicha de los que en ella mueren, la
memoria de los grandes caudillos" [10:I,85]. As is to be expected,
death is a predominant theme in these poems. Death in battle or
as a prisoner of war on the sacrificial stone is presented as being
superior to any other form of death and, therefore, is to be actively
pursued, for the soldier killed in battle and the sacrificial victim
attained the highest of Aztec heavens, becoming companions of
the Sun. Thus, the Aztec warrior-poet cries out,

> ¡Corazón mío, no temas:
> en medio a la llanura quiere mi corazón
> la muerte de obsidiana:
> sólo quiere mi corazón
> la muerte en guerra!   [10:I,217]

> For he who dies the death of a warrior
> goes before, goes to be with,
> in order to stay with the sun.   [11:107]

The Xochicuicatl, or *canto de flores,* is comparable to Western idyllic poetry, though having as its own peculiar characteristic
"la tendencia a la reflexión, y la sombra de la muerte [que] baja
leve y sutil sobre sus florecientes alegrias" [10:I,87]. The Mexican's
natural tendency toward melancholy led him to envision beside
each blooming flower one that was withered and faded. "Hay una
melancolía que domina aún entre las canciones que monotona-
mente aluden a las flores. La flor puede ser un símbolo de esta

poesía: efímera, fugaz, bella, perfumada, y, bien pronto, mudada en amarillos pétalos y en basura que arrebata el viento. Tal es la concepción de la vida y de la belleza en estos balbucientes poetas" [10:I,189].

Thus, in the following poem, behind the exquisite imagery of strings of flowers flowing from the mouth of the poet, lies the omnipresent lesson of the ephemeral nature of man, who, like the flowers of spring, lasts but a moment and is gone.

Comienzo a cantar, soy cantor:
Repártanse flores, con ellas haya placer,
con ellas haya felicidad en la tierra.

Son tu riqueza, oh cantor:
¡Feliz tú que has merecido las flores,
feliz tú que has merecido ver el canto!
Tú distribuyes a los hombres aquí
hilos de flores que salen de tu boca,
tú para ellos las has tomado:
Con ellas haya placer, con ellas haya felicidad en la
tierra.

Yo soy Yohyontzin: con avidez deseo las flores,
me vivo cantando cantos floridos.
Quiero y anhelo la amistad, la compañía, la unión:
con avidez deseo las flores,
me vivo cantando cantos floridos.

Vengo a llorar, vengo a ponerme triste,
Soy cantor y, ¿he de llevar mis flores?
¡Con ellas me ataviara yo en el Reino de la Sombra!

Vengo a ponerme triste:
¡Sólo cual flor es reputado el hombre en la tierra;
sólo por breve instante tenemos prestados flores de
primavera!
Gozad vosotros: yo me pongo triste.   [10:I,88]

Also in the canto de flores is expressed the idea of poetry, "flower and song," as a means of achieving immortality, "el guerrero daba flores de corazones; el que no era para guerra . . . daba cantos. Uno y otro perpetuaban su nombre en la tierra" [10:I,177].

We will be gone to His house,
but our word
shall live here on earth.
We will go, leaving behind
our grief, our song.
For this will be known,
the song shall remain real.
We will have gone to His house,
but our word shall live here on earth.   [3:79]

Finally, the following poem offers a philosophy shared by most poets of this genre, that life is brief and that one should neither become too attached to it nor despise it for that reason. Instead, one should be like the butterfly flitting through life, enjoying its beauty and becoming a part of it.

¿Qué es lo que meditas? ¿Qué es lo que recuerdas,
oh, amigo mío? ¿No gozas en tomar cantos?
¿No tienes el deseo de las flores del dador de vida?
    Goza junto a los tambores,
    aléjate cuando le plazca a tu corazón.

La mariposa floreciente pasa entre los hombres:
chupe la miel de nuestras flores.
Con nuestros ramilletes, con nuestros abanicos,
con el humo de nuestros cañutos se entrelaza
y persiste en deleite junto a los tambores.   [10:I,188]

Sadness and melancholy, then, pass like a fleeting shadow through the canto de flores. In the Icnocuicatl, the *canto de desolación, de orfandad*, they constitute the fundamental and almost sole themes. In this they are similar to the Western elegy, the *canto lírico*, in Spain.

Bitterness and desolation over the uncertainty of what lies ahead are clearly reflected in the following representative poems:

I, Cuauhtencoztle, here I am suffering,
What is, perchance true?
Will my song still be real tomorrow?
Are men perhaps real?
What is it that will survive?
Here we live, here we stay,
but we are destitute, o my friends!   [3:82]

¿Sólo me iré semejante a las flores que fueron pereciendo?

¿Nada mi gloria será alguna vez?
¿Nada mi fama será en la tierra?

¡Siquiera flores, siquiera cantos!
¿Ay, qué hará mi corazón?
¡En vano venimos a pasar por la tierra!   [10:I,90–91]

In each of these poems, as in the canto de desolación in general, the inanity of life and the obsession with death are constant themes.

Another theme common to this type of poetry is the life-is-a-dream aspect, so ingeniously brought to life by Calderón in Spain and, here, combined with the popular comparison of man to a flower.

"Sólo vinimos a dormir,
    sólo vinimos a soñar:
¡no es verdad, no es verdad que vinimos a vivir en la
tierra:
Cual cada primavera de la hierba así es nuestra hechura:
viene y brota, viene y abre corolas nuestro corazón:
algunas flores echa nuestro cuerpo: se marchita!" [10:I,191]

In the following poem we pass from the universal themes reflected above to a topic unique to Nahuatl poetry.

¡Sólo te busco a ti, padre nuestro dador de la vida:
sufriendo estoy: seas tú nuestro amigo,
hablemos uno a otro tus hermosas palabras,
digamos por qué estoy triste:
    busco el deleite de tus flores,
    la alegría de tus cantos, tu riqueza!

Dicen que en buen lugar, dentro del cielo,
    hay vida general, hay alegría:
    enhiestos están los atabales:
    es perpetuo el canto con el que se disipa
    nuestro llanto y nuestra tristeza:

¡es donde ellos viven, es su casa:
    ojalá lo supierais así, oh príncipes!   [10:I,192]

Here man is placed in all of his misery, before instinctively perceived, insuperable powers which leave him with a terror of his nothingness and a complex feeling of abandonment and fear, resignation and surrender, mixed all the while with a certain feeling of distrust.

The fourth category into which Garibay divides Nahuatl lyric poetry is that of religious poetry. As should be expected, given the religious background material presented earlier in the discussion of the historical bases of the death cult, death is a salient theme in this type of poetry. Constant reference is made to sacred war, sacrificial ritual, and the death of the gods and men. Thus, in the following segment from a longer religious poem, an abundant harvest is attributed to the abundant offering of sacrificial victims.

¡El humo de la hoguera! Hacen estruendo los escudos!
   ¡El dios de los cascabeles!
Allí son tremoladas tus flores, oh Enemigo,
hacen allí el estruendo las Aguilas, los Tigres.

Tú te has mostrado amigo, gracia hiciste a los hombres:
hay ondular de llamas, el polvo amarillece:
van a brotar rojas flores, se esparcen, abren su corola.

En el agua floreciente de la hoguera
está la casa de las mariposas del escudo:
allí con dardos lee, extiende la pintura
en libros de divinas flores Motecuzoma en México.
¡Sustituyó nuestro alimento con sacrificados!

Oh dios Aguila, en tu mansión imperas:
allí con dardos lee, extiende la pintura
en libros de divinas flores Motecuzoma en México.

¡Sustituyó nuestro alimento con sacrificados!   [10:I,136]

And in the following hymn sung before the ceremony of cremation, one sees the praise of death typical of this type of poetry.

"Awaken, already the sky is tinged with red,
already the dawn has come,
already the flame-colored pheasants are singing,
the fire-colored swallows,
already butterflies are on the wing."

For this reason the ancient ones said,
he who has died, he becomes a god.
They said: "He became a god there,"
which means that he died.   [3:62]

As is to be expected, given the important role which religion
played in every aspect of the lives of the ancient Mexicans, this
particular category of Nahuatl poetry often overlaps each of the
other four categories proposed by Garibay and extends also into
the realm of narrative poetry.

The last category is that of the *poema corto*, the character of
which is defined by its size rather than by its content, for, judged
by its content, it may fit into any one of the preceding categories.
In their succinctness and intimate lyricality, these poems not only
bespeak the intellectual preoccupation of their authors with the
theme of death, but also manifest a skill which renders them capable of competing with the best of the world's lyric poetry. Let
us look at a few examples of these *pequeñas joyas de poesía
lírica*, noting, as a characteristic of each, the author's persistent
preoccupation with the theme of death.

Vida de Ilusión

¿Acaso es verdad que se vive en la tierra?
¿Acaso para siempre es la tierra?
  ¡Sólo un breve instante aquí!

Hasta las piedras finas se resquebrajan,
hasta el oro se destroza, hasta las plumas preciosas se
desgarran,
¿Acaso para siempre es la tierra? ¡Sólo un breve
instante!   [12:31]

¡Animo!

¡No te amedrentes, corazón mío!
allá en el campo de batalla
ansío morir a filo de obsidiana.

Oh, los que estáis en la lucha:
yo ansío morir a filo de obsidiana.
Sólo quieren nuestros corazones la muerte gloriosa. [12:31]

Will I end as the flowers end?
Will glory avail me nothing
My passing through this world,
Shall it be dust?
Let me then be flowers
Or at least be many songs . . .
What sayest thou, o heart?
We pass this way, we do,
All in vain.   [13:34]

In each of these categories of lyric poetry, death, and what lies beyond it, is the outstanding preoccupation.

The schools of thought concerning death reflected in Nahuatl poetry appear to be essentially three in number. The first indicates an Epicurean/*Carpe diem* trend—that there is no afterlife, therefore, enjoy life on earth while you have it.

Lloro y me aflijo cuando recuerdo
que dejaremos las bellas flores, los bellos cantos.
¡Gocemos, cantemos, todos nos vamos. . . .   [12:36]

We do not come upon this earth a second time,
O Chichimecan Princes! Let us enjoy life.   [13:33]

The second school of thought displays the definite influence of traditional religious belief in life after death, but also displays a great deal of doubt and uncertainty, as Quenamican, the very name of the place of the dead, implies, "the place where those, in one way or another, live." Looking fearfully upon man's ultimate destiny, the poets of this school adopt a skeptical and questioning attitude.

Perchance, are we really true beyond?
Will we live where there is only sadness?
Is it true, perchance is it not true? . . .
How many can truthfully say
that truth is or is not there?
Let our hearts not be troubled.   [14:132]

The followers of the third school display a more positive attitude, believing in the positive power of flower and song and in the existence of a place beyond life where one might find happiness. Thus, in the following poem is displayed a confidence, not reflected in the poetry of the other two schools, that man may lift himself up and escape the ephemerality of a dreamlike world.

> Truly, earth is not the place of reality.
> Indeed, one must go elsewhere;
> beyond, happiness exists.
> Or is it that we come to earth in vain?
> Certainly some other place is the abode of life. . . .
>
> Beyond is the place where one lives.
> I would be lying to myself were I to say,
> "Perhaps everything ends on this earth;
> here do our lives end."
>
> No, o Lord of the Close Vicinity,
> it is beyond, with those who dwell in Your house,
> that I will sing songs to You, in the innermost of
> heaven.
> My heart rises;
> I fix my eyes upon You,
> next to You, beside You,
> O Giver of Life!   [14:133]

As Angel Garibay tells us, "el enigma de la muerte, inevitable y única, hemos visto poner sus sombras en todo canto de Anáhuac. Como si la obsesión del morir, elevado por el mito a la calidad de acto sacrificial, fuera la mayor que abrumaba aquellas conciencias" [10:I,195]. This obsession with death quite naturally reflected itself in ancient Nahuatl literature, and the cult of death which we see reflected today in contemporary Mexican literature is, without a doubt, at least in part, the result of and a holdover from this ancient, indigenous obsession.

The indigenous factor, though, is not the only one to be considered in determining the bases of what is referred to today as the "Mexican cult of death." The influence of the Christian death cult as brought to Mexico by the conquering Spaniards must not be ignored, nor minimized, if one is to provide a truly accurate panorama of the historical and literary bases of the Mexican cult of death.

Nuestras vidas son las ríos
que van a dar en la mar
que es el morir.

Jorge Manrique

The thought of death, which is thirst for immortality, is the
profound concern of the Spanish people.

V. S. Pritchett

2

Historical and Literary Bases of the Cult of Death in Spain

WITH THE COMING of the Spanish conquistador, the Mexican cult of death began slowly to evolve into the phenomenon which we see reflected in Mexican literature and customs today. The Spanish Catholic brought with him to the New World a Christian death cult which, in many respects, was strikingly similar to its pagan counterpart, though the basic concepts of death of these two cultures may have differed rather significantly.

The historical bases of the cult of death in Spain are far more diverse and complex than those of the Mexican phenomenon; the roots of the Spanish character, of which the cult of death is an outstanding feature, lie not only in the indigenous Iberian culture, but also in the various other cultures which over the centuries have been imposed upon that area which is today Spain. In addition to the indigenous culture, the Germanic, the Semitic, and the Arabic cultures each contributed to a certain extent to the development of the Spanish cult of death. The Greek historian Strabo, for example, long ago observed, as a marked characteristic of the Iberian, an apparent delight in suffering and death. It is an aspect of the Iberian character to which scholars and historians have alluded consistently over the centuries. As Havelock Ellis observes, "when we reflect on the history of Spain and the temperament of the Spaniard, it is difficult not to realize a certain indifference to pain, almost a love of it. The early Iberians, even when nailed to the cross, still chanted their national songs, unvanquished in spirit, to the astonishment of their Roman conquerors, and the Iberian mothers dashed their children to death rather than that they should live to be slaves" [15:43].

The centuries during which Spain pertained to the Roman Empire marked the occurrence of several events also significant to the development of the Spanish cult of death. Among these is the famous and much admired mass suicide at Sagunto in 219 B.C., when the chief men of that city, allies of Rome, threw themselves and their treasures into the flames rather than surrender to the Carthaginians. It was an act which has been emulated many times in Spain's history.

These were also the years in which Seneca developed the stoic philosophy which is so closely associated with the cult of death and which for the Spaniards merely "answered to an instinct they already felt in their veins" [15:46].

In the subsequent discussion of the cult of death, as manifested in the contemporary Mexican short story, we will see that this stoic attitude, which was, and is, an outstanding characteristic of the Spaniard, found its counterpart in Mexico and, due to the resulting fusion of these two similar attitudes, was even further intensified there. As Joseph Vélez explains, "La raza mexicana ha sido, y es, estoico por naturaleza. La actitud estoica se manifestaba ya antes de la Conquista cuando los indios eran sacrificados. Ahora que si se añade a esta actitud estoica de los españoles, se verá que la actitud azteca se refina y se manifiesta en una manera más prominente, y así ocurre" [16:46–47].

The entrance of Germanic tribes into Spain in A.D. 409 marked the beginning of a new step in Spanish history and a very significant one in the history of the cult of death. It was the Visigoths who, with the conversion of Recaredo in 589, adopted Catholicism and introduced the ecclesiastic culture into Spain. From that time on, Catholicism and the cult of death went hand in hand in Spain, for the Catholic Church provided the Spaniard with a philosophy which was delightfully compatible with his inherent fascination with death. We may trace most of the outstanding elements of the cult of death to the religious tenets of Catholicism, the contempt for terrestrial life and material values, the belief in an eternal life after death and the emphasis on the spiritual rather than the material, the preoccupation with the brevity of life and the mercurial nature of temporality, mortal corruption, and the idea of life as a dream. In short, a tendency appeared to put a far higher value on death or, rather, life after death than on life itself.

Thus, in the works of Miguel de Unamuno, one of Spain's outstanding intellectuals, one can readily discern the powerful influence of religious teachings and philosophy upon the Spanish attitude toward life and death.

A human soul is worth all the universe, someone has said—
I know not who, but it was excellently well said. A human
soul, mind you! Not a human life. Not this life.   [17:198]

The Preacher's vision of life's tragedy caught the essential
fact that everything is a dream. This "breath of Solomonic
wisdom" was infused into the Spanish mentality, along with
"a certain cult of vivifying death." The result was a kind of
popular philosophy whose central idea was "the sense of the
nothingness of everything temporal before the eternal," a
notion which "gives to our people a fortitude that shields
them against the attacks of life."   [18:269]

And, finally, speaking of the Spanish cult of death, he tells us,

And what has been the deepest wellspring of the life of our
nation but the longing to survive? For our so-called cult of
death is nothing else. It is not our cult of death, but our cult
of immortality.   [19:171]

During the seven centuries after the defeat of the Visigoths
in A.D. 711, two new cultures were introduced into Spain, the
Arabic and the Hebrew. Their influence was such that, as Angel
del Río states, "algunos reyes de Castilla, a partir de Alfonso VI,
ostentan orgullosamente el título de 'Rey de las tres religiones' "
[20:I,29].

The influence upon the cult of death of these cultures cannot
compare, however, to that exerted by the Visigoths with the introduction of Catholicism into Spain. Catholicism was, and remains,
by far the outstanding vehicle for expression of the cult of death
in the Spanish world. But the Arabs and the Jews also exerted a
certain influence upon the development of the phenomenon and
may well have contributed significantly to its intensification. As
Joseph Vélez points out, "la influencia de los moros, influencia
oriental-africana, se manifestó en las artes y en todos los aspectos
de la vida española; especialmente en la actitud hacia la vida y
hacia la muerte" [16:8].

The Spaniard's fatalistic nature, which will also be discussed
at further length in subsequent chapters, has also been attributed
to the Arabic strain in his blood, though I am inclined to agree
with scholars who trace its origins to times considerably prior to
the years of Arabic domination in Spain.

The Semitic influence upon the Spanish cult of death is essentially an indirect one in that it is in the books of the Old Testament prophets that one finds the roots of the profound Spanish
preoccupation with the *vanitas-vanitatum* theme, despite the fact
that these teachings and prophecies reached the Spanish people
through the Catholic Church and not through Judaism. Also, the
amargo-vivir sentiment, which Américo Castro sees as "caracte-
rística del hispano-hebreo" [21:525], lends itself very well to the
cult of death and may well have influenced later Christian literary production in Spain, in which manifestations of the phenomenon were clearly evident.

Basically these are the cultures and religions which together
form the historical bases of the cult of death in Spain. The phenomenon was manifest in almost every aspect of Spanish life and
culture. As was the case in Mexico, so too in Spain the artistic production of the nation reflected the preoccupation of her artists
with the theme of death. "In Spanish painting and sculpture, the
theme of death is treated again and again by every artist. The
gloom of the mortuary, the luxury of the lying in state, is their
favorite subject. The preoccupation is common in Catholic art,
but no Catholic artists in other countries have had so exclusive a
passion; it appears, also, in nonreligious painting" [22:66–67].

The phenomenon was also vigorously reflected in the nation's
literary production. In discussing the manifestations of the cult of
death in pre-Conquest Spanish literature, I shall confine my discussion again to poetry and endeavor to compare and contrast the
manifestations of the death cult in Spanish poetry to those in
Nahuatl poetry whenever possible, hoping, in this manner, to
make apparent the fusion of certain elements from both cultures
in the development of the death cult and its frequent manifestations in contemporary Mexican literature. "De siempre nos ha
llamado la atención la repetida insistencia con que el tema de la
muerte aflora en la literatura castellana. Hasta tal punto se manifiesta en todas las épocas que, sin temor a errar, podríamos cali-
ficarla como una de las 'constantes' del espíritu español. De una
forma más o menos ostensible, más o menos oculta y callada, el
sentido de la muerte aparece en la pintura, en la escultura, en la
tradición folklórica y en todas las manifestaciones de nuestro arte
culto o popular" [23:7].

Scholars of every age have noted and accepted this inherent

predilection toward the idea of death in Spain, and repeatedly they have tried to answer the question of its existence and to discover the bases of this especially Spanish predisposition, a key to the very essence of the Spanish soul and to its metaphysical foundation, which has been indelibly stamped upon its literature. In the Middle Ages, for example, death was a dominant obsession of the Spaniard. He was born under the curse of original sin, he lived in constant fear of death from hunger, battle, or pestilence, and he was doomed, even in the world to come, to suffer in the flesh the pangs of purgatory or the more enduring torments of hell. In consequence, he viewed death and its terrors with feelings alternating between fear and contempt, and he dwelt on the spectacle of corruption with fascination [24:88–89].

In literature the salient motifs which gave expression to this obsession were essentially three in number. These, as expressed by the noted historian of the Middle Ages, J. Huizinga, were as follows: "The first is expressed by the question: Where are all those who once filled the world with their splendor? The second motif dwells on the frightful spectacle of human beauty gone to decay. The third is the death dance, death dragging along men of all conditions and ages" [25:193]. Of the three, Huizinga finds that in the Middle Ages the dance-of-death, or death-the-leveler, motif and the gruesome vision of mortal corruption were by far more potent than the elegiac *ubi-sunt* motif.

Toward the middle of the fourteenth century, we see these motifs displayed in one of the most famous works of the Spanish Middle Ages, *El libro de buen amor,* by Juan Ruiz, el Arcipreste de Hita. Death is not the principal theme in this work, but it is a conspicuous one in "La muerte de Trotaconventos" (stanzas 1520–75) and in the old woman's short epitaph which follows in stanzas 1576–78.

Muerte, al que tú fieres, liévaslo de belmez;   1521
al bueno e al malo, al noble e al rehez,
a todos los egualas e lievas por un prez;
por papas e por reys non das una vil nuez.

Non catas señorio, debdo nin amistad;   1522
con todo el mundo tienes cotiana enamistad;
non ay en ti mesura, amor nin piadad,
sinon dolor e tristeza, pena e grand crueldad....

Dexas el cuerpo yermo a gusanos en fuessa;   1524
al alma que lo puebla liévastela de priessa;
non es el omne cierto de tu carrera aviessa;
de fablar en ti, Muerte, espanto me atraviessa. . . .

Fazes al mucho rico yazer en grand pobreza,   1528
non tiene una meaja de toda su riqueza;
el que bivo es bueno e de mucha nobleza,
vil, fediondo es muerto, aborrida vileza. . . .

Desprecias loçanía, el oro escureces,   1549
desfazes la fechura, alegría entristeces,
Manzillas la limpieza, cortesía envileces:
Muerte, matas la vida, el amor aborreces. . . .

Prendióme sin sospecha la Muerte en sus redes;   1577
parientes e amigos, aquí non me acorredes;
obrad bien en la vida, a Dios non lo erredes:
que bien como yo morí, assí todos morredes.   [26:408-22]

It is plainly evident in these passages that in presenting a picture of medieval Spanish society, especially its more ribald aspects, Ruiz has not ignored the medieval Spaniard's obsession with death, and his influence upon future works in which the death theme will be an important, if not the exclusive, element is immense. As is pointed out by Juan Ayuso Rivera, "Se llega a través de toda la creación popular y anónima con notas de verdadera crudeza realista—como subraya Salinas—a la primera forma expresa de elegía, dedicada a Trotaconventos por el propio Arcipreste: '¡Ay muerte, muerte seas, muerte y malandante!'

"Esto va a señalar el nacimiento de toda una serie de Plantos, Defunciones, Decires, Coplas, como los numerosos del Cancionero de Baena" [23:98].

El libro de buen amor, then, provides us with one of the first manifestations in literature of the Spanish cult of death. Even at this early stage of development of the death theme, though, we notice many similarities between this and the Nahuatl expression of the same theme, and we also notice here the basic differences in concept and interpretation of death which will ever distinguish these literatures one from the other. One expression of the death theme which we find in both literatures is that of the democratizing force of death, the idea that all persons and things shall eventually have to face death regardless of their social or economic status. We see this idea expressed often in *El libro de buen amor*. Note, for example, stanzas 1521, 1522, and 1549. And we see the same idea expressed in Nahuatl poetry, as, for example, in the following poem written in ironic praise of King Itzcóatl:

> ¡Con este canto es la marcha
> a la región del misterio!
> Eres festejado,
> divinas palabras hiciste,
> ¡Pero has muerto! . . .
>
> Por eso cuando recuerdo a Itzcóatl,
> la tristeza invade mi corazón.
> ¿Es que estaba ya cansado?
> ¿O venció la pereza al Señor de la casa?
> El Dador de la vida a nadie hace resistente . . .
> Por esto continúa el cortejo:
> ¡es la marcha general!   [27:117]

Here, though, we also notice one of the fundamental differences between these two concepts of death. In pre-Conquest Spanish poetry, this democratizing force has not only physical implications, but also moral ones. Ruiz, for example, not only warns us that all men and things are subject to physical destruction, but he also warns us that every man, despite his worldly status, may run the risk of eternal damnation if he is not ever preparing himself for death by doing good works. In this respect, the pre-Conquest Mexican concept of death was less democratic, since paradise was reserved for only a select few.

As mentioned in the preceding chapter, the doctrine of Quetzalcóatl did contain certain laws of interior preparation which seemed to indicate that behavior in life was of some consequence for the soul, but these laws were completely corrupted by the Aztecs until only the manner of a man's death bore any significance in determining his soul's destination. But nowhere in any Mexican religion did there exist the concepts of heaven and hell that exist in Christendom. The idea that man could escape death through good works would have been inconceivable for the pre-Conquest Mexican. It was only a relatively small number of these people* who could expect anything other than a journey to Mictlan and eternal nothingness, and these achieved a different fate only by virtue of their manner of death and not by virtue of any moral conduct in life. Therefore, the fundamental difference between the views of death which existed for Spanish and Nahuatl cultures as manifested in their literatures was that, for the former, the preoccupation with the idea of death seemed to stem from an attempt to escape from it through salvation, whereby, for the other, this preoccupation seemed to stem from a natural bitterness, fascination, or intellectual curiosity resulting from confrontation with and acceptance of death as part of the natural order of existence.

To try to escape this natural order was inconceivable. As R. A. M. VanZantwijk explains it, "The West European wishes to be reminded as little as possible of the concept 'death' and he imagines his own family dead even as living beings (angels) in order, nevertheless, to escape being confronted with the hard truth of death. The Aztecs perceive life and death as indivisibly bound together, and as such the one is not preferable to the other. The contradistinction which Europeans see between life and death does not arise in the Aztec train of thought. In Europe life is connected with beauty and death, with the lugubrious, the hideous; the Aztecs see only the beauty of the natural order in which life and death appear as indivisible components of progress" [7:75]. Thus, nowhere in Nahuatl literature do we find anything that approximates the moralizing tone present in Ruiz's passages on death and characteristic of Spanish moralistic poetry in general, for, just as this moralizing tone is characteristic of the pre-Conquest cult of death in Spanish literature, the lack of it is characteristic of the Nahuatl.

Also, along these same lines, we might note that the view of

---

*The soldier who died in battle or on the sacrificial stone became a companion of the sun. His hours were filled with war songs and mock battles until, after four years, he was reincarnated as a hummingbird, flying from flower to flower in the warm air. Women who died in childbirth became goddesses and accompanied the sun from zenith to setting. For those who had died of drowning or by lightning or of a disease thought to be brought about by water, such as dropsy, Tlaloc, the Rain God, had reserved a tropical paradise filled with flowers and warm rain and peaceful happiness. For the rest there was Mictlan and a four-year journey through the underworld besieged by icy winds and monsters until they finally crossed the nine rivers into Hades and vanished totally and forever. [1:107-8]

death presented by Juan Ruiz is, in general, a far more negative one than any we find in Nahuatl poetry. This again is most assuredly due to the fact that the Christian believed in the possibility of escape from death and, therefore, viewed it as something completely negative, synonymous in his mind with all that is vile, evil, and fearsome. Death was viewed as the end of all things, not as a part of a natural cyclical order of existence. It is "dolor e tristeza, pena e grand crueldad" (1522), and he who dies "vil, fediondo es muerto, aborrida vileza" (1528).

Though the fear of death is natural to all human beings, it is expressed in Nahuatl literature most often as a lament for the futility of life—an idea unheard of for the Christian, who saw life as a trial which everyone must undergo to achieve eternal life—or, in the tone of a question, as a search for the truth of what was and what would be—also out of the question for the Christian, whose religion provided him with a clear statement of the meaning of life and a detailed picture of life after death either in heaven or in hell. Nowhere in Nahuatl literature do we find the gruesome vision of mortal corruption, of worms and decay, such as we see in Ruiz and in the works of many later writers. Nor would we find reference to the abhorrent physical nature of the dead in the literature of a people who were accustomed to the sight of human sacrifice, the taste of human flesh, and the veneration of death objects in their art and in their everyday lives.

The essential difference in literary expression of the death theme between the Nahuatl and the Spanish, even in its earliest stages of development, is, therefore, clearly the result of differing concepts of the nature of death. For the Spaniard it was a vile and ugly phenomenon which could and ought to be escaped through salvation. For the ancient Mexican it was a natural phenomenon as much a part of life as life itself and devoid of any negative or positive implications such as heaven and hell. The concept of *libre albedrío*, or "free will," present in Ruiz and all moralistic poetry of pre-Conquest Spain and brought to its apogee in the works of Calderón de la Barca, is utterly lacking in Nahuatl poetry.

Half a century after the creation of *El libro de buen amor*, *La danza de la muerte* appeared. The medieval obsession with death is here painful and terrifying, and the didactic purpose of the poem is evident—to emphasize that everyone must one day face death, often an unexpected one, and that he should be ever avoiding sin or he may face eternal damnation. The poem is in the form of a vast allegory, forerunner of the more sophisticated *autos sacramentales* of the Golden Age, in which Death describes herself in all of her ugliness and calls people of various ages and social stations to join in her macabre dance.

> Yo soy la muerte cierta a todas criaturas
> que son y serán en el mundo durante;
> demando y digo: ¡Oh, honbre!, ¿por qué curas
> de vida tan breve en punto pasante?
> Pues no hay tan fuerte ni recio gigante
> que de este mi arco se puede amparar,
> conviene que mueras cuando lo tirar
> con esta mi flecha cruel traspasante.
>
> A la danza mortal venid los nacidos
> que en el mundo sois de cualquier estado,
> el que no quisiere a fuerza y amidos
> hacerle he venir muy toste priado.
> Pues que ya el fraile os ha predicado
> que todos vayáis a hacer penitencia,
> el que no quisiere poner diligencia
> por mí no puede ser más esperado.   [28:143–44]

The outstanding motifs in this poem are the dance-of-death, death-the-leveler, motif and the mortal-corruption motif. Here, as in *El libro de buen amor*, the emphasis is on the democratizing force of death and the transitory nature of beauty, wealth, and traditional, worldly values. Also analogous to *El libro de buen amor* are the strong social satire and the humor displayed in this work, though it must be noted that the humor in *La danza de la muerte* is of a far more macabre nature than that of *El libro de buen amor*, and its degree and purpose far less open to discussion.

Here we might notice another parallel between the Spanish and Nahuatl where both use poetry as a means of social protest. In the Nahuatl we see an example of this in the poem to King Itzcóatl, cited earlier in this chapter (p. 25).

During the early fifteenth century, the dance-of-death, death-the-leveler, and mortal-corruption motifs were carried on by didactic poets with little variation from the manner in which their fourteenth-century predecessors had used them as a warning to their pleasure-loving contemporaries. The *canciller* Pero López de Ayala, whose work was to greatly influence moralistic poetry for the next half century, in an early part of his *Rimado de Palacio*, presents the death-the-leveler theme in the following manner:

Bien sabes tu, por çierto, e non deues dudar,
Ca la muerte non sabe a ninguno perdonar,
A grandes e pequeños, todos quiere matar,
E todos en comun por ella han de pasar.   [29:I,94]

As flagrant corruption and striving for wealth came to characterize the reign of Juan II, the dance-of-death, death-the-leveler, motif gained new power and social significance, becoming an indispensable element in didactic poems of the period.

Hand in hand with this motif was that of mortal corruption, the loathsome vision of bodily decay and decomposition which so effectively struck fear in the hearts of the people of those times. Echoing the warning tone of the biblical prophets, López de Ayala created the following lines of his *Rimado de Palacio*:

El vno enrriqueçe, al otro va muy mal;
Despues viene la muerte, que a todos es egual,
E los cubren gusanos e cosas non les ual . . .   [29:I,128]

Sánchez Talavera uses the same theme in a *deçir* composed at the death of Ruy Díaz de Mendoza when, recalling certain prominent figures carried off by death, he states,

Todos aquestos que aqui son nombrados,
los vnos son fechos çenisa e nada,
los otros son huesos la carne quitada
e son derramados por los fonssados;
los otros estan ya descoyuntados
cabeças syn cuerpos, syn pies e syn manos;
los otros comiençan comer los gusanos,
los otros acaban de ser enterrados.   [30:III,1076]

The mortal-corruption motif also commonly took the form of a lament for feminine beauty. Note, for example, the following stanzas from *La danza de la muerte*, in which Death calls two young maidens to her dance.

A éstas y a todos por las posturas
daré fealdad la vida partida,
y desnudedad por las vestiduras,
por siempre jamás muy triste aburrida;
y por los palacios daré por medida
sepulcros oscuros de dentro hedientes,
y por los manjares gusanos royentes
que coman de dentro su carne podrida.   [28:144]

References of this type to the transitory nature of physical beauty were frequent in pre-Conquest Spanish poetry. And we see something of this same sort in Nahuatl poetry, though such references therein are achieved through comparisons of man to nature, man as the flowers, for example, rather than through graphic descriptions of physical deterioration.

The ubi-sunt motif, as we have seen, was generally far less popular during the fourteenth century than were the dance-of-death and mortal-corruption motifs. During the fifteenth century, however, this motif enjoyed a noteworthy revival, presaged at the turn of the century by López de Ayala's *Rimado de Palacio.*

A conventional element of the ubi-sunt motif, particularly popular in the fifteenth century, was the catalogue of illustrious personages of antiquity. Of this device we see an excellent example in the following deçir by Gonzalo Martínez de Medina, whose catalogue progressively moves from the great mythical and historical figures of antiquity to those of his own contemporary Spain:

    Mira que fue del grande greçiano
Alixandre, Julio e Dario e Pompeo,
Hercoles, Archiles, don Ector troyano,
Priamo e Mino e Judas Macabeo,
Dandolo, Trabo, Suero e Tolomeo,
Menbrot, Golias, el fuerte Sanson,
Vergilio, Aristotiles, el gran Godeon,
e todos los otros que en los libros leo. . . .

    Mira el d'Estuniga e el de Velasco
que ayer estauan en muy grand potençia,
e como sus fijos avien d'ellos asco
despues que la muerte mostro su presençia;
¿que pro les touo la grand exçelençia

nin rricos thesoros tan mal allegados,
castillos e villas, baxillas, estados,
que asy poseyeron con tanta femençia?   [30:II,749]

This same device is also to be found in Nahuatl poetry.

Two other elements commonly combined within the ubi-sunt motif were social satire and the melancholy vanitas-vani-tatum. Together these two created a tone of warning reminiscent of the Old Testament prophets.* The inevitable similes of life as a dream, a flower, a river, and a passing breeze recur frequently in passages of this type. This emphasis on the mercurial nature of temporality, with its underlying tone of warning, weaves thread-like throughout the poetry of the fifteenth century, from Ayala to Manrique.

Non es segurança en cosa que sea,
Que todo es sueño e flor que peresçe,
el rico, el pobre, quando bien se otea,
conosçe qu'es viento e pura sandeçe; . . .   [30:II,764]

Las justas y los torneos,
paramentos, bordaduras
    y cimeras,
¿fueron sino devaneos?
¿qué fueron sino verduras
    de las eras? . . .
¿dónde iremos a buscallos?
¿qué fueron sino rocíos
    de los prados?   [28:172]

It is here that we find one of the most marked similarities be-tween Spanish and Nahuatl poetry, for not only do we find the same emphasis on temporality, but we also find a strikingly simi-lar use of imagery in the two poetries. For example, in the Spanish poems presented above, we note the prevalence of the similes of life as a dream and life, or man, as the flowers. A marked propen-sity toward the same similes is evident in the following Nahuatl poem:

*"Etienne Gilson en 'Les idées et les lettres' ha seguido la trayectoria de esta preocupación profunda por cantar la brevedad de las cosas terrenas, y encuentra las fuentes más antiguas en Baruc (III,16–20), el Eclesiastés e Isaías" [23:99].

Sólo venimos a dormir, sólo venimos a soñar:
no es verdad, no es verdad que venimos a vivir en la tierra.

En yerba de primavera venimos a convertirnos:
llegan a reverdecer, llegan a abrir sus corolas
nuestros corazones.
es una flor nuestro cuerpo: da algunas flores y se seca.

[12:31]

The preoccupation with the brevity of life and the mercurial nature of temporality is, therefore, typical of both Nahuatl and Spanish poetry, both exhibiting a strikingly similar use of imagery to express this preoccupation. We would never find in Spanish poetry, as we do in the Nahuatl, the comparison of a sacrificial victim to a flower (see p. 13) or a popular expression of the inanity of life, which in the Nahuatl is often linked with the obsession with its brevity (see pp. 13 and 15), but we do find a definite tendency in both literatures toward melancholy. In studies of both cultures, this melancholic nature has been related to the cult of death.

Finally, there are two other elements in both pre-Conquest literatures which are of significant interest in the discussion of the cult of death. The first of these is the glorification of the soldier's death, the Spanish *buena muerte*. For both cultures, with their traditional cults of fame and stoic natures, this type of death signified everlasting renown and heavenly reward. Thus, in the Nahuatl, poems of this nature, the cantos de águilas, de príncipes, de guerra, constitute an entire category of lyric poetry. Of these we saw several examples in the preceding chapter. And in the Spanish, examples of poetry in praise of the buena muerte also abound and are particularly noticeable in the poetry of the various illustrious members of Jorge Manrique's family, as in the following section of the *Proverbios* of the Marqués de Santillana and in the last part of Manrique's *Coplas*:

Codro quiso mas vençer
que non biuir;
non refuso morir
e padesçer
por ganar e non perder
noble conpaña:
buen morir es por fazaña
de fazer.

[32:446-47]

Y pues vos, claro varón,
tanta sangre derramásteis
   de paganos,
esperad el galardón
que en este mundo ganásteis
   por las manos;
y con esta confianza,
y con la fe tan entera
   que tenéis,
partid con buena esperanza,
que esta otra vida tercera
   ganaréis.   [28:175]

Anna Krause refers to the cult of fame as "the most vital adjustment which the Spaniard of the fifteenth century made to the
problem of death, . . . the rational and heroic adjustment which
enabled the more advanced minds of the period to rise above the
negative aspect of death" [31:121, 124]. This they did to the point
whereby death, the traditional epitome of all that was ugly and
vile, was actually clothed in beauty. The parallel between Spanish
and Nahuatl poetry as it concerns this particular element of the
cult of death is very nearly exact.

Hand in hand with this glorification of the buena muerte was
the consolatory element, cultivated with special predilection in
Spanish poetry by Gómez Manrique. This poetic genre, which
preached the stoic acceptance of the death of a loved one, relieved
at last of life's trials, "urges Christian fortitude in accepting the
breves amarguras of this life that we may enjoy the delights of
the hereafter. The stoic and the Christian note are thus fused in
characteristic manner" [31:121]. Obviously the Christian element
in this type of poetry would be lacking in the Nahuatl; nonethe-
less, the stoic element was emphatically present in much of Nahuatl poetry. Stoicism in the face of the death of a loved one was
encouraged to such an extent in Aztec Mexico that there actually
existed a law prohibiting any obvious display of grief over the
sacrifice of one's child. Any negative reaction to human sacrifice
at all carried with it the strong possibility of punishment by
death.

Let us again consider the Spanish ideology. If we regard literature, in this case poetry, as the reflection of the subconscious
of its author, who is in turn the product of his culture, it seems that
the preceding references to the three motifs, dance-of-death,

death-the-leveler, mortal-corruption, and ubi-sunt, and their obvious popularity in pre-Conquest literature, as well as the popularity of the consolatory genre and the glorification of the buena
muerte, must indicate a definite preoccupation with death in pre-
Conquest Spain. To quote again J. Huizinga, "no other epoch has
laid so much stress as the expiring Middle Ages on the thought
of death. An everlasting call of *memento mori* resounds through
life" [25:138]. This statement seems to find strong literary support
in the literature of pre-Conquest Spain. Throughout Spanish literature, examples in every century attest to the fact that this Spanish preoccupation with death did not end with the Conquest. It
went on to flourish in that century and in the following one under
such exemplary poets as the sixteenth-century mystics and the
great poets of the seventeenth century, among whom, in regard
to the use of the death theme, loom prominent the figures of Que-
vedo and Calderón. It continued through the Romantics, the Nat-
uralists, and into the twentieth century until, discussing the poetry
of García Lorca, Pedro Salinas is moved to say, "Pero Lorca,
aunque expresa con originalidad y acento personal evidentes el
mismo sentir de la muerte, no ha tenido que buscarlo por procesos
de especulación interior, en las galerías de su alma. Se lo encuentra en torno suyo, en el aire natal donde alienta, en los cantares
de las servidoras de su casa, en los libros de su lengua, en las ig-
lesias de su tierra; se lo encuentra en todo lo que su persona individual tiene de pueblo, de herencia secular. Nace Lorca en un
país que lleva siglos viviendo un especial tipo de cultura, el que
llamo 'cultura de la muerte' " [33:374].

La muerte calaca y flaca—
  no engorda por más que empaca.

Popular refrain

3

The Cult of Death
as a Social Phenomenon

PATRICK ROMANELL, in *Making of the Mexican Mind,*
presents a very effective comparison of the North
American and Mexican mentalities. Franklin D. Roosevelt's
phrase "rendezvous with Destiny," he tells us, "suits perfectly a
people like ours, ever confident of achieving bigger and better
things, material and spiritual. And were we to compare the other
America's mentality with ours, the corresponding phrase which
comes closest to revealing her tragic sense of life would be that of
Mexico-inspired American poet Alan Seeger, 'rendezvous with
Death' " [34:24].

Pre-Conquest Nahuatl culture and pre-Conquest Spanish culture together form the soil in which the roots of modern Mexican
society grew and were nurtured over the centuries. The bases of
the Mexican cult of death clearly lie in these cultures. But just as a
child is born of his parents and grows to be an individual distinct
from either of his progenitors, so the contemporary Mexican cult
of death developed into a phenomenon significantly distinct from
either of those from which it was born. As Octavio Paz points out,
"la muerte mexicana es estéril, no engendra como la de aztecas
y cristianos" [35:49].

The centuries which followed the Conquest and the confrontation of indigenous and Spanish cultures saw their gradual fusion into one culture distinct from either of them, yet containing
elements of both. Death as a way of life was an element inherited
from both mother cultures and sustained by four centuries following the Conquest in which "Mexico experienced more violence to
life than any other country in the world" [36:3]. "The colonial era
was one of slow attrition and of relative peace, during which the
blood and culture of conquering Spain, imposed on the native Indian masses, fused and faded into an ethnic and cultural pattern
that after 300 years emerged definitely Mexican in stamp and

spirit" [89:xxxiv]. During this period of "relative peace," however, over 7 million members of the indigenous population perished violently or from imported disease, until, almost 300 years later, on September 16, 1810, an outcry was heard in the village of Dolores, Guanajuato, that was to initiate a series of revolutions and outbreaks which would last intermittently for over a century and which would put an end to the colonial era in Mexico. For over half a century thereafter, Mexico was wracked by war with foreign enemies and by internal strife between the warring liberal and conservative factions of the government. The Porfirio Díaz regime brought with it a period of unequaled prosperity and peace (based upon absolute suppression). By the end of this regime, the Revolution of 1910 was imminent.

The Mexican Revolution of 1910, "the only true revolution Mexico has ever had" [89:xxxvi–vii], was directed solely against the unconstitutional Díaz regime and at its outset displayed no clear-cut program for social reform. It was only after seven years of bloody contention among the various revolutionary leaders that the ideals for which the Revolution has come to stand were formulated and given official form in the Constitution of 1917.

In the two and a half decades following the outbreak of the Revolution, Mexico knew little real peace. By 1928 all of the major revolutionary leaders had been killed and a Catholic rebellion had taken place. It was not until late 1931 and the inauguration of Lázaro Cárdenas as president that Mexico began to acquire a certain amount of stability and embark upon the road to lasting peace. Since then, instances of mass violence have been on the decline, but centuries of violence have left their stamp on all aspects of Mexican life and letters, constituting an outstanding element of the New Mexican society.

As we know, literature is often the reflection of the subconscious of its author who is, in turn, the product of his culture or society. It is most important, therefore, that we define the cult of death as a social phenomenon before going on to the discussion of its manifestations in literature. Consequently, the views of several leading scholars of contemporary Mexican culture are presented in an attempt to demonstrate clearly and definitively what is meant by the term "cult of death."

In *Six Faces of Mexico*, Russell C. Ewing states that "everywhere, in the worship of the gods, in the processes of village government, in the dances and other arts, there has been and still continues a fusion of Indian and European. These mixed ways of rural life and in a large part of city life—these blends of cultural traditions—are the essential Mexico. It is often hard to tell which tradition is dominant, if either" [37:66].

As some of the prominent manifestations of the cult of death in contemporary Mexican society are reviewed, the reader should keep in mind that most of them are products of this process of fusion. For example, from their indigenous heritage of human sacrifice and of complete disregard for the individual, from their utter defeat at the hands of the Spaniards, which in their minds could only have been explainable as an act of "traición de los dioses, que reniegan de su pueblo" [35:46], and, finally, from the pitiful decimation of their people to one-seventh of the original population in a mere thirty years following the Conquest, comes the deep sense of inferiority of the Mexicans, which, in turn, leads to "fantasies in which one is a hero or a saint" [38:218]. And to become either, one must die. Therefore, one of the outstanding proofs of a man's virility in modern Mexico is "cuando afirma convincentemente o demuestra que no le tiene miedo a la muerte" [39:15]. "Death is the ultimate means to salvage prestige. The fondness for dying—Iturriaga calls it necrolatry—seems rooted in both the indigenous civilization and in Spanish culture" [38:219], in the deified sacrificial victim, but also in the Spaniard with his profound and often suicidal cult of fame. Undoubtedly from these same sources stems the ever-popular Mexican maxim, "Dime cómo mueres y te diré quién eres" [35:45].

The Mexican's attitude toward death, his indifference toward it as well as his fascination with it, is very effectively explained in the following passages by Octavio Paz who, better than any scholar today, has brought to light the true nature of the Mexican soul.

> La indiferencia del mexicano ante la muerte se nutre de su indiferencia ante la vida. . . . Nuestras canciones, refranes, fiestas y reflexiones populares manifiestan de una manera inequívoca que la muerte no nos asusta porque "la vida nos ha curado de espantos." Morir es natural y hasta deseable, cuanto más pronto, mejor. . . . Matamos porque la vida, la nuestra y la ajena, carece de valor. Y es natural que así ocurra: vida y muerte son inseparables y cada vez que la

primera pierde significación, la segunda se vuelve intrascendente. . . . Ante ambas el mexicano se cierra, las ignora. . . . [Sin embargo, la muerte] está presente en nuestras fiestas, en nuestros juegos, en nuestros amores y en nuestros pensamientos. Morir y matar son ideas que pocas veces nos abandonan. La muerte nos seduce. . . . La muerte nos atrae. Por otra parte, la muerte nos venga de la vida, la desnuda de todas sus vanidades y pretensiones y la convierte en lo que es: unos huesos mondos y una mueca espantable. En un mundo cerrado y sin salida, en donde todo es muerte, lo único valioso es la muerte.   [35:48-49]

It is not surprising, then, that in a test undertaken to measure the degree of perturbation caused by each of 100 selected words, the word "death" fell into the fifth, or minimum, range of perturbation among Mexican women tested and into the fourth range, also very low, among Mexican men [40:47].

Finally, a much noted psychological manifestation of the cult of death is the Mexican's strikingly fatalistic and stoic nature. "El estoicismo ante el dolor y la muerte" and "un sentimiento de pesimismo en el fondo del alma" [41:122, 123] were fundamental characteristics of the Aztec personality. The "famous fatalism of the race" [42:32], ascribable both to the Arabic strain in their ancestry and to an innate religious disposition, as well as Senecan stoicism, "the fundamental philosophy and almost religion of Spain" [15:45], were fundamental characteristics of the Spaniards. As Joseph Vélez points out, "un pueblo fatalista y lleno de ideas lúgubres y fúnebres, por causa de su religión, unirá su sangre y su civilización a un pueblo igualmente fatalista y estoico por causa, también de su religión. El resultado de esta fusión ya se puede adivinar sin necesidad de ser determinista" [16:14]. The result was that Aztec attitudes were refined and augmented by their Christian counterparts until they manifested themselves in a manner more prominent than either of these.

Physical manifestations of the Mexican's attitude toward death also abound in his everyday life and customs. A few of these which I have noted in my own travels in Mexico are the exceedingly sanguinary religious statuary displayed in Mexican churches—Christ, the suffering Savior, streaming with blood and clothed in gaping wounds; martyred saints graphically displaying their wounds—and the real or simulated remains of various saints, church dignitaries, or Christ Himself, presented for the viewing in glass-topped coffins, often wrapped in blood-stained gauze, in very many Mexican churches. Also, I was struck by the conspicuous presence of skulls, skeletons, mummies, or other death objects of one material or another in virtually every Mexican household and by the presence of these same objects as part of the decorations applied by bus drivers to the front section of their vehicles. (Among these the most striking object for me is the doll's head so often appearing on the shift lever of the bus, usually as a handle.) Noteworthy, too, are the frequent allusions to death in the graffiti written on Mexican trucks. And, finally, Mexican newspapers display a definite talent for graphic detail in reporting traffic fatalities, murders, or other acts of violence, while black-bordered death notices are inordinately precise and scattered conspicuously throughout each newspaper.

Another interesting manifestation of the cult of death which I have personally viewed is the mummies of Guanajuato. Here and in several other places in Mexico, the mummified remains of the dead are proudly displayed for all to see, as if to announce to the world that "el mexicano está acostumbrado a vivir codo con codo con la muerte y no la teme, antes por el contrario, la acepta y la acepta como su compañera" [16:36]. I was particularly surprised to learn from a guide with whom I discussed this rather gruesome display that the majority of the visitors to the catacombs in which the mummies are displayed are not foreign tourists, as would be expected, but, rather, Mexicans, either vacationers to the city or residents thereof. Apparently such a display is repulsive to many foreigners; certainly many Americans would find it so, but it has proven so popular among Mexicans that the mummies eventually had to be placed behind glass partitions to prohibit their being picked apart by tourists desirous of a souvenir of their visit.

Many other manifestations of the cult of death have been noted by scholars of Mexican culture. For example, Tavera notes and substantiates with Rorschach records the "morbid eagerness" of Mexican medical students [43], while others have linked to the cult of death the bullfight, the machismo syndrome, and the high rate of homicide in Mexico, "the highest culpable homicide rate of the nations of the world that keep accurate records" [36:5]. The cult of death is also effectively reflected in Mexican sayings and jokes as, for example, in the following two jokes from A. Jímenez's *Picardía mexicana:*

> —¿Te gustan las flores?
> —Sí.
> —Bueno (saca su revólver y ¡pum, pum!),
> ¡que te lleven coronas!

> —Mira, ése es mi papá.
> —¿Cuál?
> —El del sombrero de charro.
> —Los dos llevan sombrero de charro.
> —El de la camisa blanca.
> —Pero si los dos la traen blanca.
> —Te voy a indicar cual. (Apunta y ¡pum, pum!)
> El que cae.   [44:230]

But the manifestation *par excellence* of the Mexican cult of death is the national celebration of the Day of the Dead on November 2. "Tan acostumbradas están las gentes a la presencia constante de la muerte que sus ritos y ceremonias son manifestaciones de su actitud" [16:35]. "Candies and pastries in the form of skulls, toy coffins, and funeral processions of paper figurines are among the many macabre playthings on sale for the festival" [38:219]. "Comemos el día de los Difuntos panes que fingen huesos y nos divierten canciones y chascarrillos en los que ríe la muerte pelona" [35:49]. In many parts of Mexico, specifically in those in which there is still a strong Indian tradition, this celebration, "a convenient adaptation of an ancient Indian Day of the Dead called *Tzi kin*" [45:88], is of a full month's duration, the greatest ceremony being on November 2. On this day, it is believed, the dead are permitted to come to earth to visit their relatives, partake of the spirit of food and gifts brought to them at their final resting places, and warm themselves over the candles and fires kept burning there. W. E. Garrett explains the ceremony as it takes place in the cemetery on Janitzio Island in Lake Pátzcuaro. "Shortly after midnight, on November 2, the island women bring to their family burial plots an assortment of gifts, food, candles, marigolds,* and

---

*The marigold, it might be noted, called the "flower of the dead," is also a solar symbol, and, therefore, well attests to the dualistic nature of the celebration—that is, that it is a product of both pagan and Christian tradition.

wooden frames decorated with flowers, fruit and small skulls molded of sugar. They spread mats on the ground and set up the decorations—one candle for each remembered relative and a censer of burning copal. They arrange the food and sprinkle marigold petals over the entire setting. Then the women and children sit in contemplation or chant prayers throughout the chill night. . . . 'Salga, salga, salga, . . .' a fisherman chanter implores a departed soul" [46:146, 181–85].

The cult of death is very much alive today in the minds of the Mexican people. I present as final proof of this the following words of one of these people, a poor Indian with no formal education, though he is today's most popular and well-known Mexican "philosopher," Juan Matus, the *brujo* whose teachings have inspired four best-selling volumes by Carlos Castaneda. This is what don Juan, as a "man of knowledge" and a living compendium of Mexican thought and culture, tells us about death:

By the time knowledge becomes a frightening affair, the man also realizes that death is the irreplaceable partner that sits next to him on the mat. Every bit of knowledge that becomes power has death as its central force. Death lends the ultimate touch, and whatever is touched by death indeed becomes power. . . . Thus, to be a warrior, a man has to be, first of all, and rightfully so, keenly aware of his own death. But to be concerned with death would force any one of us to focus on the self, and that would be debilitating. So the next thing one needs to be a warrior is detachment. The idea of imminent death, instead of becoming an obsession, becomes an indifference.   [47:182–83]

"How can anyone feel so important when we know that death is stalking us?" he asked. . . .

"The thing to do when you're impatient," he proceeded, "is to turn to your left and ask advice from your death. An immense amount of pettiness is dropped if your death makes a gesture to you, or if you catch a glimpse of it, or if you just have the feeling that your companion is there watching you. . . ."

He replied that the issue of our death was never pressed far enough. And I argued that it would be meaningless for me to dwell upon my death, since such a thought would only bring discomfort and fear.

"You're full of crap!" he exclaimed. "Death is the only

wise adviser that we have. Whenever you feel, as you always
do, that everything is going wrong and you're about to be
annihilated, turn to your death and ask if that is so. Your
death will tell you that you're wrong, that nothing really
matters outside its touch. Your death will tell you, 'I haven't
touched you yet.'"   [48:55]

From the discussion of the background and nature of the cult
of death in Mexico and its early manifestations in literature, I
now turn to the other basic topic of consideration indicated in the
title of this study, the Mexican short story. In the following chapter, I will deal with several of the outstanding contemporary authors of this genre.

Los seres humanos mueren todo el tiempo, a cada instante, en cada rincón. Al morir, al tener que morir, ya han muerto, ya recuerdan su muerte futura, anticipan su muerte pasada, mueren su vida presente.

Ariel Dorfman

True life nourishes itself on death and renews itself second by second, in a continuous creation. A life without any death in it, without any unpiling in its continual piling up, would be a perpetual death, the repose of a stone. Those who do not die do not live; those who do not die at every instant, to rise from the dead on the instant, do not live.

Unamuno

Todo al fin es muerte . . . distintos modos de morir.

Clara Passafari

4

Manifestations of the Cult of Death in the Contemporary Mexican Short Story

W E HAVE SEEN that the bases of the cult of death lie in both the pre-Conquest indigenous and the pre-Conquest Spanish cultures and that the result of the fusion of these cultures was that the cult of death became an even more prominent aspect of the new Mexican society, to the point where we find it still very much alive today and one of the outstanding social phenomena of contemporary Mexico. As would be expected, literary manifestations of the cult of death abound, not only in pre-Conquest Mexican and pre-Conquest Spanish literature, but also in the most recent works. As Aguiles Nazoa points out, "Entre los signos adversos a que algunos pueblos de América acogieron las expresiones de su animismo colectivo, ninguno iguala como poder omnipresente a ese sombrío Numen de todo lo mexicano, que se llama la Muerte" [49:163].

It has also been observed that one of the newest and most successfully cultivated literary genres in Mexico is the short story and that many of the best writers of the country are at this time turning their attention and talents to the cultivation of that genre which, according to Seymour Menton, "al cumplir cien años, ha llegado a tal grado de perfección que está en una meseta de la cual no sé si va a seguir subiendo" [50:51]. Let us, therefore, turn our attention now to a study of the manifestations of the cult of death in this new and powerful genre, the contemporary Mexican short story.

I have chosen to limit my discussion of the topic to the years 1947–60. During these years, there arose in Mexican literature a group of authors whose writings indicate a conscientious attempt on their part to uncover certain outstanding aspects of *mexicanidad* and, in some cases, to search out their roots in indigenous culture and to illustrate the degree to which ancient customs and attitudes have influenced the contemporary Mexican attitude toward life and death. Invariably in their attempt to uncover the Mexican soul, these authors have been led to deal with the cult of death.

In this chapter, we shall be examining the manifestations of this phenomenon in the short stories of six authors, Juan Rulfo, José Revueltas, Rosario Castellanos, Guadalupe Dueñas, Carlos Fuentes, and Eraclio Zepeda. Of these six, several have achieved international renown and are considered among Mexico's most famous and skilled writers. Others have enjoyed considerable fame within Mexico. And all but the youngest of these have participated in the "Los narradores ante el público" lecture series in Mexico City. They do differ, though, in the degree to which the short story has influenced the fame of each as a writer. Of these six, José Revueltas, Rosario Castellanos, and Carlos Fuentes owe their fame primarily to the novel; yet, they have also written many excellent short stories and are generally included in the best collections of the genre. Guadalupe Dueñas and Eraclio Zepeda, on the other hand, owe their fame entirely to one volume each of short stories, while Juan Rulfo owes his fame equally to the short story and the novel, his entire literary production consisting of one outstanding work in each genre. There is no question that Juan Rulfo is one of Mexico's greatest writers of short stories. He is also the greatest single exponent of the cult of death in Mexican literature, a fact which is hardly surprising if we consider the following details of his personal history.

Rulfo is a native of Jalisco, the state in which each of his short stories is set, and although some fellow writers and critics, such as Juan José Arreola, may express feelings to the contrary, the majority of critics seem to feel that his physical descriptions of the Jaliscan southwest are quite accurate. The cult of death manifested in his short stories is to some extent, then, a direct result of the physical environment in which Rulfo was born and raised. "The landscape . . . is decrepit. The living are surrounded by the dead. . . . Most people have migrated. Those who have stayed behind are there to keep the dead company. 'Their ancestors tie them to the place. They don't want to leave their dead.' Sometimes when they move, they actually dig up their graves. 'They carry their dead on their shoulders.'* Even when they leave them behind, they continue to bear their weight" [51:249–50].

Rulfo himself is by no means free from this weight as is attested to by his obsession with tracing the genealogy of his family, a second point of interest in his personal history. A brief look at this genealogy suggests another motive for Rulfo's being such an outstanding literary spokesman for the Mexican cult of death, for lives of violence and early death abound in the Rulfo family tree. As Rulfo tells us,

> A mi padre no lo mató un peón, no tenía peones, y eso lo ha afirmado erróneamente Seymour Menton en su libro *La cuentística iberoamericana*. . . . Lo mataron una vez cuando huía . . . y a mi tío lo asesinaron, y a otro y a otro . . . y al abuelo lo colgaron de los dedos gordos, los perdió . . . todos morían a los treinta y tres años.   [52:viii–ix]

> En la familia Pérez Rulfo, nunca hubo mucha paz; todos morían temprano, a la edad de treinta y tres años y todos eran asesinados por la espalda. Sólo a David, el último, víctima de su afición, lo mató un caballo.   [53:65]

From this family tradition and from the regional and national tradition of which it was a product, *El llano en llamas* was born, a collection of fifteen short stories published in 1953. Certainly death was a "constant companion" of Juan Rulfo as he wrote the stories of *El llano en llamas*. The setting, the characterization, and the action of each of these is infused with manifestations of the cult of death. In some of them though, one of these elements, either setting, characterization, or action, manifests this phenomenon particularly well. I have chosen to discuss three short stories from the collection which I feel best utilize one of each of these elements as a vehicle of expression of the cult of death. These are, for its use of setting, "Luvina"; for characterization, "La Cuesta de las Comadres"; and for action, "El llano en llamas."

Richard M. Eastman, in *A Guide to the Novel*, makes the following observations concerning the setting of a fictional work: "Through the techniques of thematic or symbolic imagery, the novelist may select some physical detail of his story and so im-

---

*Being quoted is Rulfo himself.

pregnate it with thematic associations that whenever that detail recurs, it embodies that theme" [54:59]. Juan Rulfo, in the stories of *El llano en llamas*, has made a microcosm of the Jaliscan southwest, and he has so impregnated that setting with thematic associations that it embodies the theme of death. The villages and the landscape depicted in these stories are, in the words of the author, "like graveyards dedicated to the cult of death" [51:266].

Among the fifteen stories of *El llano en llamas*, the example par excellence of Rulfo's use of setting as a vehicle of expression of the Mexican cult of death is "Luvina," the name of a village which is, in the words of the narrator, a onetime resident of the place, "el purgatorio. Un lugar moribundo donde se han muerto hasta los perros y ya no hay ni quien le ladre al silencio" [55:104]. Luvina is little more than a ghost town in which fertility has become sterility and from which the truly living have long ago fled, leaving behind only a small group of spectral, unhappy figures— bat-like figures who "pass by like shadows," "esposas sin maridos, . . . niños sin infancia, . . . viejos sentados en el umbral de las puertas, esperando la muerte" [56:48]—tied to their dead and themselves more dead than alive. Nothing lives in Luvina. A black mountain wind does not even let the *dulcamaras* grow, "esas plantitas tristes que apenas si pueden vivir un poco untadas a la tierra, agarradas con todas sus manos al despeñadero de los montes" [55:94]. "Todo el lomerío pelón, sin un árbol, sin una cosa verde para descansar los ojos; todo envuelto en el calín ceniciento. Usted verá eso: aquellos cerros apagados como si estuvieran muertos y a Luvina en el más alto, coronándolo con su blanco caserío como si fuera una corona de muerto" [55:95].

Luvina is the home of sadness and despair, a place where the dead "live" and the living are "dead," and where the few withered human beings who remain there refuse to flee and leave behind their dead. "Pero si nosotros nos vamos," they say, "¿quién se llevará a nuestros muertos? Ellos viven aquí y no podemos dejarlos solos" [55:103]. And besides, to the outside world, these people are already dead. "No saben si existen," the narrator explains, and the only time their existence is recognized is when the government sends someone to Luvina to fetch and kill one of its residents who has done something wrong.

Therefore, surrounded on all sides and from within by death, they sit and wait, "sentados en sus puertas, con los brazos caídos.

. . . Sólos, en aquella soledad de Luvina" [55:102]. "Nadie lleva la cuenta de las horas ni a nadie le preocupa cómo van amontonándose los años. Los días comienzan y se acaban. Luego viene la noche. Solamente el día y la noche hasta el día de la muerte, que para ellos es una esperanza" [55:101].

The comparison is often drawn between Luvina and Comala, the setting of Rulfo's novel *Pedro Páramo*. It seems certain that in creating Luvina Rulfo was paving the way for the creation of Comala, a village of real ghosts. As Hugo Rodríquez Alcalá points out, " . . . si Comala es un pueblo de muertos, de fantasmas, Luvina es un pueblo de vivos que apenas viven. . . . Comala existe fuera del tiempo o, mejor en un tiempo eternizado. Luvina también existe fuera del tiempo. Allí 'todo se queda quieto, sin tiempo, como si se viviera en la eternidad.' . . . Si en Comala hay sólo fantasmas, los hombres y mujeres de Luvina parecen fantasmas. El narrador nos cuenta: 'Vi a todas las mujeres de Luvina con su cántaro al hombro, con el rebozo colgado de su cabeza y sus figuras negras sobre el negro fondo de la noche' " [56:48–49].

In "Luvina", time is of little significance. As Ramón Xirau tells us, "Luvina se acerca, más que ningún otro, a la negación total del tiempo" [57:4]. Or as James Irby says, "Todo parece estar suspendido en el tiempo, casi muerto, sólo esperando el lento desmoronar de las cosas que acabará al fin con la existencia. Como en todos los relatos del Rulfo, el tiempo—dimensión con la cual se mide la acción humana—ha perdido su significado. No hay pasado ni futuro, sólo hay un presente eternamente agonizante. Lo explica el narrador anónimo: 'Me parece que usted me preguntó cuántos años estuve en Luvina, ¿verdad? . . . La verdad es que no lo sé. Perdí la noción del tiempo desde que las fiebres me lo enrevesaron; pero debió haber sido una eternidad. . . . Y es que allá el tiempo es muy largo. Nadie lleva la cuenta de las horas ni a nadie le preocupa cómo van amontonándose los años . . .' " [58: 140–41]. Thus, there appears to be little difference between the timeless world depicted in these stories and the dead world depicted in *Pedro Páramo*.

As in other stories of the collection, such as "Macario" and "Es que somos muy pobres," there is no actual human death depicted in "Luvina." And yet, setting and atmosphere clearly insinuate the presence of death. "Buen número de los cuentos de *El llano en llamas* no puede eludir la presencia de la muerte, y

'Luvina' . . . va a mostrar una nueva manera de tratarla por las in-
sinuaciones propias del ambiente y del aire particular de sus hombres subsumidos en él. El sobrecogimiento que invade el ánimo
en una relectura de 'Luvina' es por la presencia de la muerte"
[59:13].

The same atmosphere present in "Luvina" is present throughout the entire collection. For as Emmanuel Carballo points out,
"Rulfo es un cuentista monocorde que expresa un mundo angosto
en el que todos los lugares—los escenarios—son más o menos
iguales" [60]. His is a world "desprovisto de sentido y orden,
donde las cosas suceden fatalmente, porque sí, escapando a cualquier explicación lógica o racional; un mundo hostil en el que
está desterrado, impotente, el hombre" [58:135], a world "dedicated to the cult of death" [51:266].

Setting, though, is often primarily a reflection of the psyche
of the characters in a given literary work, as several outstanding
literary theorists have pointed out. For example, Wellek and Warren state: "Setting is environment, and environments . . . may be
viewed as metonymic, or metaphoric, expressions of character. A
man's house is an extension of himself. Describe it and you have
described him. . . . Setting may be the expression of a human will.
It may, if it is a natural setting, be a projection of the will. Says
the self-analyst Amiel, 'A landscape is a state of mind.' Between
man and nature there are obvious correlatives" [61:221].

The cult of death is a social phenomenon, a psychological
phenomenon, and is therefore best reflected in people and their
actions. Let us, therefore, turn to the discussion of a story in which
characterization serves as the outstanding vehicle of expression of
the phenomenon: "La Cuesta de las Comadres."

The story is essentially an account, in the first person, of the
killing of Remigio Torrico whom the narrator, an old friend of
the Torricos, stabbed through the navel and heart with a harness
needle. It is an emotionless, though graphic, account of an act
which we cannot help but feel should arouse more emotion. But
it is precisely the lack of emotion displayed herein which makes
this story such an excellent portrayal of the typical Rulfian hero.
In the persons of the narrator and the other characters to whom
he introduces us, we find embodied most of the attitudes so often
associated with the cult of death and so often reflected in all of
Rulfo's works—stoic resignation, fatalism, insouciant violence.

The narrator accepts impassively the Torricos' murder of the mule driver, and he displays no emotion in his description of the deaths of the Torricos, one at his own hands. And perhaps even more significantly, he does nothing to avert the situation which brings about the death of Remigio, when a simple explanation of the facts as he knew them might have done just that. Rulfo's characters in this story, as in so many others, are conspicuously lacking in free will, and their stoic acceptance of their situation reflects itself not only in their attitude toward life, but also in their attitude toward death. The ultra-passive attitude which the narrator and the other characters of "La Cuesta de las Comadres" assume in the face of acts of violence and their failure to act to prevent them reflect the nonchalance of a people "for whom death is always close and life has little value" [51:260].

Speaking of the Rulfian hero in general, Raúl Chávarri tells us, "Los héroes de Rulfo son siempre héroes pasivos . . . los héroes menos heroicos que pueden encontrarse. No hay en ellos la serena actitud de revelarse [sic] contra la fortuna, no se 'toman las armas contra un piélago de calamidades,' sino que simplemente se sufre esto que los ocurre" [62:175]. Thus, the people of the hill of the *comadres* do not resist the tyranny of the Torricos, two men against fifty-eight; they simply leave their lands never to return. "Se iban callados la boca, sin decir nada ni pelearse con nadie. Es seguro que les sobraban ganas de pelearse con los Torricos para desquitarse de todo el mal que les habían hecho; pero no tuvieron ánimos. Seguro eso pasó. La cosa es que todavía después de que murieron los Torricos nadie volvió más por aquí. Yo estuve esperando. Pero nadie regresó" [75:22].

As Diane Hill points out, the "matter-of-fact" tone which his characters display "nos dice mucho sobre la perspectiva de Juan Rulfo; no sólo su perspectiva literaria, sino también su actitud hacia el hombre individual. El hombre no es más que otro elemento del mundo. No tiene más importancia ni más significado que los demás componentes de la realidad. . . . Este efecto se logra mediante una actitud ultrarealista, en la que la descripción de una muerte o la de un árbol son iguales en su falta de sentimiento. El árbol y la muerte participan, ambos, de una sola realidad; de modo que ni el uno ni la otra tiene más importancia dentro del esquema general de esa realidad. El mundo existe por sí mismo, como entidad objetiva, y la presencia o falta de un árbol

más o un hombre más no lo altera ni lo afecta profundamente"
[63:338]. The narrator tells us that when he gave the dead mule
driver one last kick, "sonó iqual que si se la hubiera dado a un
tronco seco" [75:25]. And somehow we feel that the comparison is
well drawn.

Exterior character description is conspicuously lacking in all
of Rulfo's stories. We know, for example, that Remigio Torrico
had only one eye, "black and half-closed," but, aside from that,
we know nothing of the physiognomy of the characters in "La
Cuesta de las Comadres." And, yet, with characteristic verbal
economy, Rulfo provides us with such a vivid impression of the
attitudes and ways of life of his characters that we see them better than if they had been described to us in detail. It is as if we
view his characters from the inside out, rather than from the outside in. And the outstanding element of their personalities viewed
from this perspective is their attitude toward life and death.

If we bear in mind the earlier discussion of the historical
bases of the cult of death, we will note more than a small rem-
nant of indigenous philosophy in the attitudes of Rulfo's characters, especially here in "La Cuesta de las Comadres"—the lack of
concern for the individual, the acceptance of death as a part of
the natural order of existence with no apparent concern for its
redeeming quality or for the Christian concept of repentance and
salvation. And, yet, the phenomenon displayed herein is far more
than a simple holdover of ancient indigenous attitudes. It is the
product of years of fusion and social development. It is that modern phenomenon described earlier and so effectively by Octavio
Paz (p. 39), a phenomenon based upon years of tradition and,
yet, in itself unique.

Many have accused Rulfo of *tremendista* techniques, his
stories being steeped in blood, violence, and death. But as José de
la Colina points out, "su creación bebe en una fuente inexhausta
de la tradición mexicana, . . . [donde] se encuentra ese mismo tono
directo, sencillo, cortado, para hablar de la crueldad como de una
cosa cotidiana y común, y de la muerte que le puede suceder a
cualquiera, en cualquier momento. El mexicano se siente sumer-
gido en un mundo indiferente y cruel, en el que la vida, . . . 'no vale
nada' " [64:136].

And, finally, we should allude to one factor common to the
lives of all of the characters in *El llano en llamas*, the state of soli-

tude in which they all live. Octavio Paz relates the solitude of the Mexican to his fascination for death and to his propensity toward seemingly senseless acts of violence. Violence, as he sees it, is a means by which the Mexican escapes the solitude of his every-day life, and it is often his only means of communicating with his fellow man, or, more accurately, it is a natural result of his inabil-ity to do so. Thus, instead of communicating the facts of his brother's death to Remigio Torrico, the narrator of that story kills him. The fascination which death exerts over the Mexican, Paz tells us, is also perhaps the result of his hermit-like solitude and of the fury with which he breaks out of it [45:39–54].

"La Cuesta de las Comadres" well illustrates Rulfo's use of characterization as a vehicle of expression of the Mexican cult of death. But it is only representative of a number of stories which might have been cited. As Claude Couffon points out, "En la mayoría de los personajes de Rulfo, la muerte está escondida, dis-puesta a brincar o brincando. Ella es la consecuencia lógica de esta violencia que atormenta todas las mentes, una violencia inútil por cierto, pero para estos seres toscos, sin educación, parece la única manera de exorcizar la realidad: el hambre, el aislamiento, la falta de trabajo, la inclemencia de la naturaleza" [65:47]. For Rulfo's characters and, as has been noted previously, for many Mexicans, violence and death are "the ultimate means to salvage prestige."

George D. Schade well sums up the relationship of charac-terization and the cult of death in El llano en llamas: "Rulfo peels many of his characters down to the core, but some of them, like the landscape, frequently clouded over and hazy, remain blurred, imprecise, and taciturn figures. They are never seen in full face, but always in a silhouette, like the lugubrious, black-garbed crones of 'Luvina.' The one thing standing forth clear and ubiqui-tous is death—overpowering life—which seems to hold scant value in this world" [66:x].

In El llano en llamas, character and setting combine to create a picture of a world which is static, timeless, and always hostile toward man, who has somehow learned to become either indiffer-ent or resigned to it. It is a world in which action of any sort seems futile, for all of life in the world of El llano en llamas is predeter-mined and any action on the part of any character to try to alter or improve his world is destined to failure. The only "action" in these stories consists of various senseless and fruitless acts of violence, acts which are born rather from a feeling of indifference toward life and death than from any sense of purpose, other than revenge.

In a world in which living is often a static, meaningless experience, dying is often the only real form of action. As Alfonso León de Garay states, "morir es siempre una forma disponible de actuar, no de esperar" [67:59]. But even these acts are usually nothing more than senseless manifestations of repressed hostilities due to years of suffering and inertia. Thus, James Irby tells us of *El llano en llamas*, "No hay acción; los personajes no hacen nada. Hasta las muertes que éstos infligen cruelmente a sus semejantes parecen ser actos ajenos a su voluntad y ellos sólo los vehículos obedientes de una ira que desciende como un rayo del cielo. He aquí, pues, las dos constantes que rigen el vivir y el morir en el mundo de Rulfo: pasividad ensimismada y violencia inexplicable" [58:149].

Action in the short stories of Juan Rulfo, then, if it exists, invariably takes the form of violence and death and thereby serves as another vehicle of expression of the Mexican cult of death. Let us again look at a story to illustrate this point.

"El llano en llamas," the story which gives the collection its name, is the longest story therein and also the one in which we find the most action in the usual sense of the word. It is a story of the Mexican Revolution, but the Revolution here has lost the epic quality displayed in many of the great works it inspired. All that remains in Rulfo's story is the senseless death and destruction it engendered. As El Pichón, narrator of the story, and his comrades set out again to join Pedro Zamora after a brief defeat-inspired peace, he tells us, "Seguimos caminando de frente, encandilados por la luminaria de San Buenaventura, como si algo nos dijera que nuestro trabajo era estar allí, para acabar con lo que quedara" [55:73]. Here is a case of violence inspiring violence with no further purpose. "Era más fácil caer sobre los ranchos en lugar de estar emboscando a las tropas del gobierno" [55:76].

Then later we witness the cruel *juego del toro* in which Pedro Zamora playing the bull and armed with his razor-sharp sword playfully executes his prisoners. There is a sense of cold-blooded indifference to human suffering in the scene which especially distinguishes it. There is also the train wreck in which so many soldiers and their women die, the consequences of which had not been foreseen by Zamora's men and fill them with fear. "No sabíamos bien a bien lo que iba a suceder" [55:80], Pichón tells us, and we realize that throughout the story there is a complete lack of concern for human life and that the action displayed therein is blind and meaningless. Only death seems to have any real control over life. "En todos los lugares triunfa la muerte, la cruel muerte mexicana que encuentra su representación simbólica en el cadáver del 'Chihuila' atejonado detrás de un madroño, con la cobija envuelta alrededor del pescuezo, y que 'parecía estar riéndose de nosotros, con sus dientes pelones, colorados de sangre' " [65].

And, finally, the manner in which El Pichón relates the most atrocious acts, as if they were the most normal, commonplace events, attests more than any other aspect of the story to the existence of a cult of death.

But there is another interesting aspect of the work. I have alluded earlier to the Mexican's strikingly fatalistic and stoic nature as a much noted psychological manifestation of the cult of death. In most of Rulfo's works, feelings of despair, hopelessness, and pessimism emanate from this fatalism and stoicism; this explains in part their lack of conclusions and their often circular quality.

"El llano en llamas" is the only story in the collection in which the typical Rulfian pessimism seems to have been tempered significantly. It is the only story in which there is a conclusion in the strict sense of the term. El Pichón is redeemed from his life of banditry and starts out upon a new life with the woman who has waited for him during his years in jail and with their son who, although he shares his father's name and a certain meanness of look, "no es ningún bandido ni ningún asesino. El es gente buena" [55:84]. "El llano en llamas," then, reminds us that the cult of death, if viewed from a national rather than a Rulfian perspective, does not by its very nature imply a completely negative outlook toward life.

The three stories discussed above well illustrate Juan Rulfo's use of setting, characterization, and action as vehicles of expression of the Mexican cult of death in the stories of *El llano en llamas*. My choice of stories to illustrate the use of each of these elements has been more or less arbitrary; as in most of the stories of the collection, the cult of death is manifested simultaneously in each. As George Schade tells us, "The elements of the harsh physical environment combine with the Mexican Indian's fatalism to forge almost a symbiosis of man and landscape. The parched, dry plain is overwhelming. The Indian accepts life as it is there, and his acts are almost inevitable. . . . Impotence and despair reign, and death rattles in the scorching air, the howling wind, the throttling dust of the plain" [66:xiv].

It is true that Rulfo expresses only certain elements of the cult of death in Mexico. We see little of the more positive manifestations of the phenomenon—the friendly humor with which death is often treated, the gaiety surrounding certain festivals and attractions in which death is the main object of festivity, the beauty of death-inspired art, etc. Rulfo presents to us only its more somber elements—psychological elements such as resignation, stoicism, fatalism, pessimism, and physical elements such as violence and death by violence. But Rulfo's style, limited as it may be, faithfully reflects the world in which his stories are set, the world of the Jaliscan *campesino*. And his stories, in general, reflect faithfully a phenomenon which dates back to the first indigenous myth of creation. As Arturo Torres-Ríoseco points out in reference to Rulfo's novel *Pedro Páramo*, "The cult of death occupies a luminous spot in Mexican mythology, and in modern times death is considered merely the inverse of life. In Mexican painting, from Posada to Orozco and Montenegro, the skeleton is an omnipresent figure. Entire books have been written on the skull in Mexican art. Such vital artists as Diego Rivera and Alfaro Siqueiros maintain constant contact with death. It should not surprise us then that an author like Juan Rulfo should choose a village of corpses as a setting for his novel" [68:83]. Neither should it surprise us therefore that Rulfo chose a village like Luvina for the setting of one of his short stories or that the cult of death occupies a luminous spot in each of the stories of *El llano en llamas*.

Rulfo is, as Reinaldo Arenas comments, "el escritor más admirado y el autor mexicano que mayor prestigio ha adquirido en la literatura occidental" [69:113-28]. Certainly his fame is due in part to the style and artistry of expression displayed in his works. But in greater part I feel that his popularity is due to the fact that Rulfo's stories reflect a national phenomenon which is in essence a key to the understanding of the Mexican soul; the reader not only sees but feels that phenomenon as Rulfo causes him to enter

the soul of his characters and to view the world from their perspective and to become, for a short while at least, a part of that
world. No other writer better suits our discussion of the manifestations of the cult of death in the contemporary Mexican short
story, for Rulfo is certainly the outstanding exponent of that phenomenon in literature.

But the cult of death is a nationally felt and expressed phenomenon and is by no means limited to the works of one author.
I therefore turn to a discussion of manifestations of the cult of
death in the short stories of several other outstanding figures of
Mexican literature.

It has been noted that all of Rulfo's works are set in Jalisco,
the state in which he was born and raised. For this reason, critics
have sometimes accused him of displaying only a limited, regional
view of Mexican life. José Revueltas was born in the city of Du-
rango and was raised and educated in Mexico City; yet, one notices several striking similarities between his works and Rulfo's,
especially in regard to the cult of death. Examination of some of
Revueltas' more recently written short stories will help to establish that the cult of death is by no means a regional phenomenon and that it manifests itself in the short stories of writers from
all regions of Mexico.

Revueltas is best known as a novelist. His second novel, *El
luto humano* (1943), won the Premio Nacional de Literatura and
made its author an internationally acclaimed literary figure. His
next work, published in 1944, was a collection of short stories entitled *Dios en la tierra*, and this too received considerable critical
acclaim. Since then short stories by José Revueltas have been included in the best anthologies and collections of the Mexican
short story and appear consistently in leading Mexican journals.
In 1960 Revueltas published another collection of eight short stories, similar in thematic content to *Dios en la tierra*, entitled *Dormir en tierra*. It is with the manifestations of the cult of death in
a number of the stories from this collection that I shall concern
myself.

Clara Passafari de Gutiérrez tells us that *Dormir en tierra*
"aborda el tema raigal de la muerte y su formidable sentido y
gravitación sobre el destino de los hombres" [70:161]. Death is certainly a central theme in most of the short stories of *Dormir en
tierra*, but outstanding among these as a vehicle of expression of

the cult of death is the second story of the collection, "La frontera increíble."

In this story Revueltas examines the transitional state between life and death, "el sitio preciso de la transición reveladora y demoníaca entre la vida y la muerte" [71:44]. The reader of this story views death from two perspectives, that of the living, in this case the family of the dying man and the priest who administers the last rites, and that of the dying man himself, and he sees that the two perspectives are irreconcilable—that there comes a point after which communication is impossible between the living and the dying, though the dying person be still technically alive. Thus, the family's concept of their loved one's death is considerably different from that of the dying man himself. "Nada alteraba el silencio recogido y humilde de la habitación. Los párpados quietos del agonizante hacían pensar que su muerte iba a ser tranquila, sin sufrimiento, no como esas muertes angustiosas en que la casa se llena de terror y hay un deseo tremendo de que todo ocurra de una vez, sin transiciones, para que cese el espectáculo intolerable del moribundo que gime o grita como una encarnación del espanto" [71:39]. To those who observed his death, it seemed a peaceful one, but revealed from within the subconscious of the dying man, it is seen to be quite another thing.

> Testimonio, cuerpo mío, duéleme, que eres mi último sufrimiento antes de que me entregue al sufrimiento puro, al que no tiene principio ni fin, ni mezcla de alegría ni de esperanza.
> [71:42]

> El cuerpo del agonizante, en el paroxismo del dolor, empezó a asirse a él, al agonizante, a abrazarlo con rabia, con una angustia no experimentada jamás. El moribundo amaba y despreciaba esta lucha, esta ruptura alta, horrible y oscuramente bella.   [71:44]

The dying man is able to perceive the living, but he is in a different world now, totally alone, and he can no longer communicate with them. As he explains it, " . . . como todos los hombres aún no tocados por la luz de la muerte, aquellos no tenían entre sí otro medio de comunicación que la palabra. Su territorio era la palabra. Su patria era la palabra. Su habitación era la palabra. Pero nada más. ¿Cómo comunicarles, entonces, la verdad de la muerte, si él poseía ahora un lenguaje extraño y antiguo, no comprensible para nadie sobre la tierra? . . . el impenetrable idioma de la muerte" [71:42–43]. Thus, the last paragraph of the work states, "En medio de su dolor, todos experimentaron una cierta tranquilidad melancólica, pues la muerte, como lo imaginaran, había sido suave, dulce, sin sufrimiento alguno" [71:45].

In "La frontera increíble," one is able to observe the feelings of guilt, remorse, and fear of the living and their misinterpretation and misunderstanding of the physical and emotional state of the dying man; one is also able to perceive the thoughts and reactions of the dying man as he enters that *frontera increíble* which separates him forever from the living who surround him. Thus, the story, a most interesting and original study of the act of dying, is a fine manifestation of the cult of death in the contemporary Mexican short story.

"Lo que solo uno escucha" expresses many of the same themes as "La frontera increíble," loneliness, lack of communication, and death. It is a beautiful story of the swan song of a small-time Mexican violinist, Rafael, who finds himself suddenly playing as he has never played before. "Los trémolos, patéticos y graves, vibraban en el espacio con limpidez y diafanidad sin ejemplo, los acordes se sucedían en las más dichosas y transparentes combinaciones, los arpegios eran ágiles y llenos de juventud. Todo lo mejor de la tierra se daba cita en aquella música; las más bellas y fecundas ideas elevábanse del espíritu y el violín era como un instrumento mágico destinado a consumar las más altas comuniones" [71:107].

Rafael's happiness is profound; yet, an inborn fatalism and stoicism prevent him from revealing his feeling to anyone, and his happiness reveals itself merely as "un aire estúpido," a look which leads his family to ask him if he is sick. In the fatalistic world in which Rafael and his family live, happiness is "un pecado que no se puede confesar," and any revelation of such feelings only causes feelings of alarm on the part of those to whom they are revealed.

"¿Estás enfermo?" preguntaron a coro y con ansiedad los niños. Rafael no respondió sino con su sonrisa lastimera y lejana.

"No les diré una palabra. Lo que me ocurre es como un

pecado que no se puede confesar." Y al decirse esto, Rafael sintió un tremendo impulso de ponerse en pie y dar a su mujer un beso en la frente, pero lo detuvo la idea de que aquello le causaría alarma.   [71:106]

As Edmundo Valadés points out, "el hombre revueltiano está destinado a lo peor" [72:22]. While Rafael is joyously thinking to himself of the beautiful change which will now take place in his life, his wife is seeing in her husband's look the undeniable omen of death. "Ahora cambiará todo," Rafael says to himself. "Será todo distinto. Todo cambiará" [71:104]. But his wife is thinking "ese brillo humilde en los ojos y esa dulzura torpe en los labios . . . es un anuncio de la muerte. No puede ser sino la muerte. ¿Pero cómo decírselo? ¿Cómo darle consuelo? ¿Cómo prepararlo para el pavoroso instante?" [71:106].

Rafael is now like the protagonist of "La frontera increíble," a dying man, though he himself does not know it, and, therefore, communication between him and his wife is no longer possible. "Toda comunicación profunda entre sus dos ánimas se había roto ya" [71:106]. Thus his wife says one thing and means another, and Rafael's feeble attempt to express his feelings is interpreted merely as a sign of drunkenness. Revueltas' characters, like Rulfo's, are completely lacking in free will. Therefore, Rafael, with no signs of protest, allows himself to be led to his bed where he dies. In a fatalistic world, it seems, happiness and death invariably go hand in hand.

"Los hombres en el pantano" is a different type of story. It is the story of a patrol of Mexican-American soldiers in World War II, trapped in a swamp somewhere in the Pacific, playing a life-or-death game of hide-and-seek with a patrol of Japanese. The first paragraph of the story explains essentially all of the rest. "La cuestión era escuchar algo vivo, y todos esperaban que este anhelado acontecimiento se produjera una vez más, de cualquier modo y como fuese, después de las dos ocasiones, ya tan lejanas al parecer, en que había ocurrido y en que esto los hizo respirar con un alivio cínico, puro y ruin, ahí metidos como estaban, con el agua cenagosa hasta el pecho" [71:49].

In the static world depicted in this story, death, the death of another, serves as a type of proof of life for those who remain. "Se trataba únicamente de oírse, de oírse nada más, y no importaba que el grito representara una baja japonesa o norteamericana, sino que todos supieran, mediante ese grito, mediante esa muerte, que cada uno de ellos no estaba solo ni muerto sobre la superficie de la tierra" [71:50]. And movement and sound, life as it were, signify death. " . . . algún imprudente o loco se había movido, . . . produciendo un rumor asombrosamente claro, preciso, increíble ahí en el pantano donde aquello significaba la muerte. . . . los hechos no eran sino testimonios, un modo de vivir, un modo de atestiguarse cada uno a sí mismo con la muerte" [71:50-51].

The static world described in the following quotation—a world in which life is a living death and death and violence are the only manifestations of life—displays an unmistakable resemblance to the static world described in the short stories of Juan Rulfo. " . . . ya no eran seres reales, . . . habían dejado de ser hombres y no podían encontrar ninguna otra manifestación de vida sino en la muerte: . . . lo único humano y viviente que les quedaba en la existencia era el aullido de los que morían, . . . la única acción viva que les estaba permitida, era la acción de matar" [71:55].

In the discussion of the manifestations of the cult of death in the short stories of Juan Rulfo, several elements were pointed out which are outstanding therein and are consistently referred to by critics as characteristically Rulfian—elements such as fatalism, stoic resignation, lack of free will, and solitude—elements in Mexican literature associated with the cult of death and evident in the setting, characterization, and action of the short stories of *El llano en llamas*. The following comments are by two outstanding critics of José Revueltas' works, but they might well have been said also of the works of Juan Rulfo, and they attest to the fact that Revueltas too, in a manner similar to Rulfo's, manifests in his short stories the Mexican cult of death. James Irby, for example, observes that the works of José Revueltas are characterized by "un materialismo estático y muerto y un fatalismo atroz que anulan acción y movimiento y crean personajes unilaterales, sin desarrollo interno, meras figuras." And he tells us that "en la obra de Revueltas se crea a menudo un ambiente denso y sofocante, misterioso y oscuro, un ambiente que las más de las veces evoca la miseria, el pathos, el terror y la soledad" [58:113]. Alí Chumacero notes that Revueltas' characters emerge from "una región demasiado hecha de una pieza, entera y uniforme, como descendida de una voluntad ajena, separada del hombre mismo. Así la volun-

tad humana resulta nacida de una fuerza muy otra que la con-
ciencia. No obedece a propio impulso ni actúa por propia con-
vicción" [73:5].

When speaking of the short stories of *Dios en la tierra* and
Revueltas' works in general, James Irby refers to certain outstanding themes—misery, desperation, sex, infirmity, hatred, terror, and
death [58:122]. These same themes persist in the stories of *Dormir
en tierra*, with one of the outstanding themes being that of death.
Death is the central theme of the three stories discussed herein,
and it is present in each of the remaining stories of the collection;
for example, life as a living death and early suicide are depicted
in "La hermana enemiga," the story of a young girl victimized by a
step-sister who makes her ashamed of her sex and who finally
drives her to commit suicide, a suicide which is almost anticli-
mactic in view of the life she had been leading. "Agotada y tem-
blorosa se puso en pie y caminó hasta el centro de la habitación,
donde, quieta y muda, quiso pensar en la muerte con toda su
alma, pero le fue imposible pues era como si ya hubiese muerto
irremediablemente desde antes" [71:82].

In "El lenguaje de nadie," an ignorant Indian buries his old
mistress alive, thinking her dead of typhus, and when she beats
upon the coffin in an attempt to free herself, he assumes that it is
her spirit which is trying to frighten him and he buries her none-
theless. His act is judged a product of ignorance by the court before which he appears, but in consequence he is forced to sign
over the piece of land which has been left to him in the old
woman's will.

Each of these stories, as well as the others of the collection, attests to the fact that manifestations of the Mexican cult of death
do exist in, and are an outstanding feature of, the short stories of
José Revueltas.

To further illustrate the contention that the cult of death is by
no means a purely regional phenomenon and that it manifests itself in the short stories of writers from various regions of Mexico,
we move south to the state of Chiapas and to a discussion of the
short stories of Rosario Castellanos.

Rosario Castellanos, like José Revueltas, is best known as a
novelist. Her novels *Balúm Canán* (1957) and *Oficio de tinieblas*
(1962) have been translated into several major world tongues. Her
poetry, too, has received considerable attention. Of her short

stories, though, little has been written in the way of critical material, although they are invariably included in the outstanding collections of the genre in Mexico and appear often in leading Mexican journals. *Ciudad Real,* published in 1960, is a collection of ten stories and is described on the back cover of the book as being "un retrato fiel de esta ciudad chiapaneca, más fiel aún por no ser una casual imagen fotográfica, sino la aguda percepción del sitio expresada con hábiles recursos artísticos; la autora colaboró con los antropólogos y los médicos que luchan por resolver los problemas de la región, y fruto de sus experiencias es este tomo en que recrea el mundo de los indígenas, de los ladinos" [74].

Although manifestations of the cult of death appear in only three or four stories of this collection, those which do appear provide a faithful image of the phenomenon as it exists in that region of southern Mexico. The second story of *Ciudad Real,* entitled "La tregua," particularly well suits our discussion. The cult of death depicted in this story is that of pre-Conquest Mexico, untainted by Christian teachings.

When a stranger, a *caxlán,* or "white man," arrives in Mukenjá—ostensibly to solicit help from the residents, as he is obviously sick but unable to communicate his purpose to them since he speaks a different language—he is immediately assumed by the Indian woman Rominka to be the disguised wandering spirit of "el *pukuj,* dueño de los montes, dueño de todas las cosas," the bringer of madness, the killer of children. Rominka, after begging for her life, runs to her hut where she encloses herself with all of her children except one whom she sends for the men. The men, in their turn, also assume that the stranger must be a harbinger of death, in the form either of a revenue agent or of the dreaded god, for both, to the Indians of Mukenjá, forced by their poverty into illegally producing and distributing *aguardiente,* signify death. They think back to when the Secretario Municipal, Rodolfo López, and his men, inconvenienced by their long search for the source of the bootleg aguardiente which had been affecting legal sales, apprehend the Indians responsible for its production and burn them in their huts. " ... cuando la paja comenzó a arder y las paredes crujieron y quienes estaban adentro quisieron huir, Rodolfo López los obligó a regresar a culatazos. Y respiró, con el ansia del que ha estado a punto de asfixiarse, el humo de la carne achicarrada" [74:33].

But an innate fatalism and stoic resignation forbid the men any thoughts of flight. "Cualquiera de las dos posibilidades era ineluctable y tratar de evadirla o de aplazarla con un intento de fuga era un esfuerzo malgastado. Los varones de Mukenjá afrontaron la situación sin pensar siquiera en sus instrumentos de labranza como en armas defensivas. Inermes, fueron de regreso al caserío" [74:34].

So the men return to their village to face whatever awaits them there. The sight of the weakened stranger, unable to stand, and Rominka's repetition of the word "pukuj" excites in them a mad thirst for revenge over this power who brings sickness, famine, and death to their village.

> Pukuj. Por la mala influencia de éste que yacía aquí, a sus pies, las cosechas no eran nunca suficientes, los brujos comían a los rebaños, las enfermedades no los perdonaban. En vano los indios habían intentado congraciarse con su potencia oscura por medio de ofrendas y sacrificios. El pukuj continuaba escogiendo sus víctimas. Y ahora, empujado por quién sabe qué necesidad, por quién sabe qué codicia, había abandonado su madriguera y, disfrazado de ladino, andaba las serranías, atajaba a los caminantes. . . . Los varones requirieron lo que hallaron más a mano para el ataque: garrotes, piedras, machetes. Una mujer, con un incensario humeante, dio varias vueltas alrededor del caído, trazando un círculo mágico que ya no podría trasponer. Entonces la furia se desencadenó. Garrote que golpea, piedra que machaca el cráneo, machete que cercena los miembros. Las mujeres gritaban, detrás de la pared de los jacales, enardeciendo a los varones para que consumaran su obra criminal.
> [74:35]

But the truce brought about by the blood of "el pukuj" is of short duration, and soon the Indians turn again to thoughts of blood sacrifice. " . . . la tregua no fue duradera. Nuevos espíritus malignos infestaron el aire. Y las cosechas de Mukenjá fueron ese año tan escasas como antes. Los brujos, comedores de bestias, comedores de hombres, exigían su alimento. Las enfermedades también los diezmaban. Era preciso volver a matar" [74:36].

In this story of a small Chiapan Indian village, we see reflected and perpetuated the attitudes toward life and death of the pre-Conquest Mexican, fatalism, stoic resignation, and the belief in blood sacrifice as a requisite for the prolongation of life. The cult of death manifested herein is little different from that of pre-Conquest, Aztec Mexico.

In the other stories of *Ciudad Real*, death is a less prominent theme, but in several of these a sense of indifference toward death, especially on the part of the Indian population, is evident. When Mariano Sántiz Nich's eleven-year-old son dies in "Arthur Smith salva su alma," "su indiferencia exasperó a Arthur" [74: 173]. The only thing that their new religion seems to have brought to these Indians is a more concrete hope for the alleviation of their suffering after death. "Mi hijo mayor está en el cielo. Allá no hay hambre, no hay frío, no hay palo. Allá está contento," says Mariano, but this hope does little to attenuate his indifference toward life and toward the physical aspect of death.

In "La rueda del hambriento," the nurse, Alicia, seems to be the only person who feels any concern for the life and death of a new-born Indian child. "El pukuj se está comiendo a mi hijo," says the child's father, and neither he nor the child's grandfather make any attempt to go and get the money which would save the child's life. Nor is the doctor willing to volunteer sustenance for the child, because he believes, and rightly so perhaps, that in that way he will never gain the Indians' respect and esteem.

And, finally, in "Cuarta vigilia," "la niña Nides" is completely indifferent when she murders an innocent Indian in order to insure the secrecy of the hiding place of her money which she never spends.

The theme of death is not omnipresent in the stories of Rosario Castellanos as it is in those of Juan Rulfo and José Revueltas, but it is present in isolated stories. "La tregua," for example, displays the cult of death as it appears today in many of the backward Indian villages of Mexico, where attitudes toward life and death are still a direct holdover from those of their inhabitants' most remote ancestors.

Sharing with Juan Rulfo the title of most prestigious Mexican writer is Carlos Fuentes, an internationally renowned and prolific novelist, short-story writer, and critic. Rulfo himself, when asked in one of his rare interviews, "¿Qué autores mexicanos destacaría usted?", replied with customary modesty, "A Carlos Fuentes. El es la base de toda literatura joven actual de México. Todos quieren ser como él. Pero no es fácil, ya que Fuentes, cuando comenzó a escribir, poseía una cultura muy amplia" [75:3]. In Miguel Donoso Pareja's opinion, "Carlos Fuentes con-tinúa siendo en México el Sumo sacerdote de la literatura juvenil, refiriéndonos a la prosa naturalmente. . . . ha sabido mantenerse a la cabeza de los narradores mexicanos jóvenes" [76:12].

Fuentes' fame, like that of José Revueltas and Rosario Cas-tellanos, rests most heavily upon his novels. These have been translated and acclaimed the world over. But Fuentes' first work, published in 1954, was not a novel, but a collection of six short stories entitled Los días enmascarados. Ten years later he pub-lished another volume of seven short stories, Cantar de ciegos. Aside from these two volumes, he has written innumerable stories for publication in leading national and international journals and anthologies.

Of his second volume of short stories, Cantar de ciegos, Rich-ard Reeves, in a bibliography of Fuentes, states that "these pieces demonstrate a significant departure from those in Los días enmas-carados in their lack of thesis and emphasis on entertainment. Several characters are typical mid-twentieth-century types who are universal in their interests rather than national or Mexican" [77:610]. But it has also been pointed out that "en todos los cuentos está presente un agudo pesimismo, un notorio desprecio hacia el ser humano y un evidente desencanto de la vida" [78:38].

Despite the presence of such elements though—elements often associated with the cult of death—the universal, cosmopolitan quality of these stories renders them less applicable to the discus-sion of our topic than those of Fuentes' first volume, Los días en-mascarados.* My discussion of the manifestations of the cult of death in the short stories of Carlos Fuentes will, therefore, focus upon two stories from that work. This first volume is also more significant as it marks the direction of much of Fuentes' later work.

The six stories of Los días enmascarados, with the exception of the second, "En defensa de la Trigolibia," which is of a purely political nature, are a combination of realism and the purest fan-

*The title of this work, Los días enmascarados, alludes to the last five days of the Aztec year, the "nemontani," "cinco días sin nombre, días vacíos durante los cuales se suspendía toda actividad—frágil puente entre el fin de un año y el comienzo de otro" [79:iv]. It also brings to mind Chapter II, "Máscaras mexicanas," of Octavio Paz' El laberinto de la soledad [35], by which Fuentes is said to have been influenced, especially. in the writing of this volume.

tasy. The first of these, entitled "Chac Mool," is considered by the author and by most critics to be the best of the collection. The story is retrospective; it begins at the end, and, little by little, it works backward to reveal the central incident upon which it is built.

Its beginning strictly adheres to logic. "Hace poco tiempo, Filiberto murió ahogado en Acapulco" [80:55]. And there appears to be a logical explanation. "Claro sabíamos que en su juventud había nadado bien, pero ahora a los cuarenta, y tan desmejorado como se le veía, ¡intentar salvar, ya medianoche, un trecho tan largo!" [80:55]. It is not until halfway through the story, as the narrator proceeds with his reading of Filiberto's diary, that the fantastic element is introduced into the narrative, to the point where, by the end of the story, it has completely overshadowed the realism of the first portion of the work.

Filiberto, a collector of pre-Columbian artifacts, purchases a statue of Chac Mool, the Aztec god of rain, in a Mexico City flea market, the Lagunilla, and upon returning home places the statue in his basement. Shortly afterward, the basement mysteriously floods, returning the Chac Mool to its legendary natural element and giving to the statue a slimy, fleshy appearance which no efforts on Filiberto's part are able to erase. Still there appears to be a logical explanation; "este mercador de la Lagunilla me ha timado. Su escultura precolombina es puro yeso, y la humedad acabará por arruinarla" [80:61]. But from this point of the narrative on, reality fades and fantasy takes over as Chac Mool takes on a living form, appears to Filiberto, and gains complete control over him. In a last effort to escape his captor, Filiberto flees to Acapulco, where he is drowned.

Even to the last page of the story, one is able to apply a logical explanation to the events recounted in Filiberto's diary—the man was mad! But the ending defies all logical explanation, and fantasy reigns triumphant. The narrator returns Filiberto's body to his home, perplexed by what he has read in his friend's diary.

Antes de que pudiera introducir la llave en la cerradura, la puerta se abrió. Apareció un indio amarillo, en bata de casa, con bufanda. Su aspecto no podía ser más repulsivo; despedía un olor a loción barata; su cara, polveada, quería cubrir las arrugas; tenía la boca embarrada de lápiz mal aplicado, y el pelo daba la impresión de estar teñido.

—Perdone . . . no sabía que Filiberto hubiera. . . .
—No importa; lo sé todo. Dígale a los hombres que lleven
el cadáver al sótano.   [80:67]

Chac Mool is not the fantastic hallucination of a madman,
but a reality who avenges himself by taking Filiberto's life before
he loses his own. Fuentes, in a brief plot summary of his story,
states that Chac Mool chased Filiberto from his home to meet his
death in Acapulco and that "in the end the owner replaces the
god in the flea market" [51:286].

The presence of death as a theme is obvious in "Chac Mool"
from the first line to the last. Here again, as in the stories of Rosario Castellanos, we see an expression of the cult of death of pre-
Conquest Mexico. Chac Mool's powers have not been diminished
by modern civilization. He is still capable of commanding human
sacrifice, of imposing ancient ritual upon modern civilization, and
of divesting man of his free will. As Emmanuel Carballo points
out, Chac Mool represents "el empuje de la sangre indígena sobre
la española, el peso de lo antiguo sobre lo moderno" [81:16]. " 'The
past, in Mexico,' says Fuentes, 'weighs heavily, because although
the Conquerors, the Spaniards, carried the day, Mexico, because
of its particular political and historical makeup, has given the final
victory to the conquered. . . . Here the defeated have been glori-
fied. Why? Because Mexico is a country where only the dead are
heroes. . . . Our heroes are heroes because they were sacrificed.
In Mexico the only saving fate is sacrifice. . . . The nostalgia for
the past in Mexico is a direct result of the original defeat' " [51:
284]. Thus, Fuentes expresses the important influence of the cult
of death upon modern Mexican society.

The world presented in "Chac Mool" is a curious mixture of
both pre-Hispanic and modern Mexican elements. To quote Emmanuel Carballo, "los hombres que pueblan este universo se de-
baten entre dos teogonías que en vez de excluirse se complemen-
tan: la azteca y la católica" [82,I:xxx]. Early in this story Fuentes
observes the complementary nature of these two religions upon
which modern Mexican society is based.

> . . . si no fuera mexicano, no adoraría a Cristo, y—No, mira
> parece evidente. Llegan los españoles y te proponen adores
> a Dios, muerto hecho un coágulo, con el costado herido cla-
> vado en una cruz. Sacrificado. Ofrendado. ¿Qué cosa más

natural que aceptar un sentimiento tan cercano a todo tu ceremonial, a toda tu vida? . . . Figúrate, en cambio, que México hubiera sido conquistado por budistas o mahometanos. No es concebible que nuestros indios veneraran a un individuo que murió de indigestión. Pero un Dios al que no le basta que se sacrifiquen por él, sino que incluso va a que le arranquen el corazón, ¡caramba!, jaque mate a Huitzilopochtli! El cristianismo, en su sentido cálido sangriento, de sacrificio y liturgia, se vuelve una prolongación natural y novedosa de la religión indígena. Los aspectos de caridad, amor y la otra mejilla, en cambio, son rechazados. Y todo en México es eso, hay que matar a los hombres para poder creer en ellos.   [80:58]

Here, then, we find that the cult of death is not only manifested in the characterization and action of the story, but is also examined from the sociological point of view. Fuentes stresses the all-important role of the cult of death as the common denominator between the Mexican and Spanish cultures which enabled their relatively effortless fusion and provided the basis for modern Mexican society. As Emir Rodríguez Monegal points out, "el mismo Fuentes ha subrayado su intento de explorar en ellos [the short stories of *Los días enmascarados*] la supervivencia de viejas culturas en el mundo mexicano" [83:146]. Undoubtedly, the outstanding feature of these old cultures was the cult of death. It is therefore the survival of this phenomenon which is often reflected in Fuentes' works.

Very similar to "Chac Mool" is the fifth story of the collection, "Por boca de los dioses." Once again, a work of art gains control of the protagonist and brings about his death. Oliverio, aficionado of painting, engages in an argument with his friend don Diego over the merits of a work of modern art by Tamayo, displayed in the entrance of the Palacio de Bellas Artes. As a result of that argument, Oliverio rips the mouth from the painting and in response to old don Diego's objections, throws him from a window to be smashed on the pavement below. As he leaves the building with the stolen mouth, he sees a beggar woman who appears to be the reincarnation of the colonial painting which don Diego had preferred and admired. Eventually, the mouth superimposes itself upon Oliverio's and gains control of him, forcing him to do things which he does not want to do. It leads him to a basement where there are many Indian gods. Oliverio flees and locks himself in his room, but he is followed there by the goddess Tlazol whom he has met before in the hotel, and she kills him after biting off the Tamayo mouth which had adhered itself to his.

"Por boca de los dioses" contains a plethora of situations and events symbolic of modern Mexican society which Fuentes often openly censures. He censures, among other things, the violent, pugnacious, and yet impotent nature of the Mexican, a nature which has previously been linked to the cult of death. He describes Mexico as an "armazón suntuoso de la carne muerta, oscura, pantanosa que va chupando palabras y quehaceres" [84:271].

Beatriz Espejo y Díaz interprets the overriding symbol of this story as being "el gran arraigo que ejercen sobre nosotros el arte y la teogonía indias" [84:272]. But the tone Fuentes imparts in this story, and to a lesser degree in "Chac Mool," indicates an air of disapproval of the cult of death, which is in contrast to the essentially objective presentation of the phenomenon in the short stories of the other authors discussed herein. Fuentes criticizes the fatalism, impotence, and meaningless violence of Mexican society. His works are a call for action as opposed to stoic resignation. Fuentes' predilection toward the theme of death attests to the degree to which the cult of death is an inherent part of his culture. But by his apparent censuring of certain elements of the phenomenon, he surpasses his contemporaries, who generally manifest the phenomenon in their literature but fail to dissect it and examine it with the critical eyes of the sociologist as does Carlos Fuentes.

The fame of two of the authors in this chapter is based exclusively upon the short story. One of these is Guadalupe Dueñas. As she states, "Publiqué en 1958 un libro de cuentos que alcanzó cierto éxito y desde entonces no he publicado para no opacar mi fama" [85:360]. The title of that one book of short stories is *Tiene la noche un árbol* which, in 1959, won for its author Guadalajara's Premio José María Vigil for having been judged the best book of the year. Since then, stories by Guadalupe Dueñas have been included in more than a dozen anthologies, and they have appeared very frequently in all of the literary journals of Mexico and in the most important newspapers of the country. She is a collaborator in the journal *Abside* and in other journals and magazines with large circulations. Her works in journals of other Latin American

countries and of Spain are numerous; some of her stories have
been translated for United States journals, and her stories are
being translated into English for publication by an important London publishing house.

Of the twenty-five short stories included in *Tiene la noche un
árbol*, the one which is most often included in anthologies is "La
historia de Mariquita," one of the many stories of the collection
which strongly manifest the cult of death. It is the story of Mariquita, first-born of five sisters, and her rather bizarre family with
whom she lives for twenty years, encased in a chile bottle filled
with a mixture of aguardiente and caustic soda, for Mariquita had
died at birth. The story is narrated by the eldest of her four sisters.
It relates how the girls' father installed Mariquita in her liquid
environment shortly after her death, and how it was decided that
her permanent abode should be in the room of her sisters, in order
to avoid the questions and disapproval of visitors. As is indicated
by the first two lines of the story, Mariquita's influence upon the
lives of the other members of her family is immense. "Nunca supe
por qué nos mudábamos de casa con tanta frecuencia," her sister
tells us. "Siempre nuestra mayor preocupación era establecer a
Mariquita" [86:23]. Thus we see that in Guadalupe Dueñas' world,
too, the dead weigh heavily upon the living.

After the death of their parents, the girls continue to move
from house to house, finally renting an old, decaying estate which
they find most agreeable and to whose supernatural inhabitants
they soon accustom themselves. "La casa se veía muy alegre; pero
así y todo había duendes. En los excepcionales minutos de silencio ocurrían derrumbes innecesarios, sorprendentes baileteos de
candiles y paredes, o inocentes quebraderos de trastos y cristales.
Las primeras veces revisábamos minuciosamente los cuartos,
después nos fuimos acostumbrando, y cuando se repetían estos
dislates no hacíamos caso" [86:26].

But Mariquita is a problem. On her account, her innocent sisters have become the objects of malicious gossip, and she herself
is accused of haunting the neighborhood. "Las sirvientas inven-
taron que la culpable era la niña que escondíamos en el ropero:
que en las noches su fantasma recorría el vecindario. Corrió la
voz y el compromiso de las explicaciones; como todas éramos
solteras con bastante buena reputación se puso el caso muy
difícil. Fueron tantas las habladurías que la única decente resultó

ser la niña del bote a la que siquiera no levantaron calumnias"
[86:26–27].

Her sisters seek a solution to these problems, but in the mean-
time, Mariquita's upkeep is terribly neglected. "Mientras tanto
la criatura, que llevaba tres años sin cambio de agua, se había sentado en el fondo del frasco definitivamente aburrida" [86:27]. So,
finally, after twenty years, Mariquita is buried in the garden of the
old estate. But she is not forgotten:

> Ahora hemos vuelto a mudarnos y no puedo olvidar el
> prado que encarcela su cuerpecito. Me preocupa saber si
> existe alguien que cuide el verde Limbo donde habita y si
> en las tardes todavía la arrullan las palomas.
> Cuando contemplo el entrañable estuche que la guardó
> viente años, se me nubla el corazón de nostalgia como el de
> aquellos que conservan una jaula vacía; se me agolpan las
> tristezas que viví frente a su sueño; reconstruyo mi soledad
> y descubro que esta niña ligó mi infancia a su muda com-
> pañia.   [86:27]

Many of Guadalupe Dueñas' stories tell of childhood en-
counters with death. In addition to "La historia de Mariquita,"
there is, for example, the story of "El moribundo," in which the
narrator recounts as her most enduring childhood memory the
long suffering and death of a beloved friend who contracted tu-
berculosis while in prison for giving aid to the Cristeros. Upon
the request of his family, long-time friends of her parents, he has
come to spend his dying days in her home. The story provides not
only a graphic description of the young man's slow demise, but
also masterfully describes a young girl's first encounter with
death.

"El sapo" and "Los piojos" are stories of the naïve sadism of
children as they inflict death by torture upon the creatures for
whom the stories are named. Two of the stories of the collection,
"Tiene la noche un árbol" and "Al roce de la sombra," combine
death and intrigue. In "Al roce de la sombra," for example, a
young girl is murdered because she witnesses the mad pleasures
of the two elderly and impoverished sisters with whom she has
come to live.

"Judit" is the story of a young girl whose excessive pride
causes her to devise a suicide pact with her boyfriend by which
she intends to triumph over interfering townsfolk.

¿Por qué doblegarse? Ella no era bien de Ramiro, ni de nadie, para que la tomaran cuando les viniera en gana. ¿Qué sabían de su conveniencia? ¿Por qué le decían que por su bien? Nadie hubiera dicho una palabra si se le hubiera ocurrido voluntariamente ser de Ramiro; también eso estaba en el orden de las cosas.

—Que hagan su gusto. Seré de él, pero no aquí. Moriremos los dos. ¡Nos hubieran dejado hablar! Aman su ruido, quieren decidir por nosotros, ser más que nosotros. No les importa más que el acontecimiento, que si yo cediera, igual los decepcionaría; en cambio, así les daremos la gran función. Por mucho tiempo hablarán de los dos.   [86:118–19]

But, as she holds the dead Ramiro in her arms, pride and self-love provide her with the rationalization she needs to excuse herself from carrying out the pact. "Es mejor que yo viva para prolongar el dolor de tu muerte" [86:121]. "Judit" is essentially a story of pride, and as such, it well illustrates the point that in Mexico pride and death very often walk hand-in-hand.

Finally, in "Las ratas" and "Guía en la muerte," Guadalupe Dueñas deals with the age-old theme of mortal corruption, the fate of the body after death. In the former, an ex-caretaker in the Panteón de Dolores describes the efficiency of the rats of the pantheon as they devour, upon arrival, the dead who inhabit the place. The final paragraphs of this story present the narrator's twentieth-century statement of the death-the-leveler motif:

Doy una moneda al hombrecillo y procuro que mis dedos no toquen su mano. Lo veo alejarse. Su estatura no es mayor que cuando sentado lustraba mis zapatos, como si no tuviera muslos y las rodillas fueran pegadas a la caja del cuerpo; arrastrando los pies camina igual que un mono de cuerda.

Miro mis manos, mis manos perfumadas, la piel que cuido y que también será devorada, repartida en sus lívidas panzas manchadas de jiote; yo que me amo tanto y que evité el contacto del pobre bolero.   [86:107]

"Guía en la muerte" is not a fictional work, but rather an account of the guided tour through the catacombs of Guanajuato where thousands go every year to view the mummies.

In speaking of the short stories of Guadalupe Dueñas, Emmanuel Carballo has stated that they are "más producto de la espontaneidad que de la reflexión" [82,I:xxi]. It has also been stated

that "la autora decanta las circunstancias y suprime toda 'esceno-
grafía' accesoria, tratando de ofrecer al lector únicamente lo esencial" [87:132]. In nearly half of the stories of *Tiene la noche un
árbol,* "lo esencial" is death. The fact that the expression of this
theme is a spontaneous one on the part of the author serves as further evidence that the cult of death is still an integral part of the
Mexican psyche and that, as such, it is freely manifested in Mexican literature.

Eraclio Zepeda, at thirty-six years of age, is the youngest of
the short-story writers to be discussed herein. His fame, like that
of Guadalupe Dueñas, rests upon one volume of short stories, *Benzulul,* published in 1959. Like Rosario Castellanos', his stories are
set in the primitive world of Chiapas, though Enrique Congrains
Martin is of the opinion that Zepeda surpasses Castellanos with
his "capacidad innata para captar lo que es esencialmente indígena" [87:212].

As an exponent of the Mexican cult of death, Zepeda also
surpasses Castellanos. For, as we have seen, manifestations of the
cult of death are evident in only selected stories of *Ciudad Real,*
while death is a prominent theme in each of the eight short stories
of *Benzulul.* To quote the back cover of the volume,

> *Benzulul* encierra una variada colección de psicologías
> primitivas, y no es casual que la muerte sea el común deno-
> minador de los ocho cuentos: el autor ha escogido esa luz fú-
> nebre por creer que con ella destacarán mejor los rasgos
> esenciales de nuestro rostro más antiguo.
> Ya que para el lector son evidentes, sobre todo, los valores
> humanos y literarios del volumen, tal vez no será inútil se-
> ñalar que también tiene interés antropológico esta sentida
> investigación del alma indígena.   [88]

The eight stories in this collection may be divided into three
categories. The first of these contains four stories, "Benzulul,"
"Vientooo," "Quien dice verdad," and "Patrocinio Tipá," in which
Zepeda describes the feelings and attitudes of the indigenous population of southern Mexico. The next category deals with characters and life styles which are typically *mestizo.* Into this category
fall "El Caguamo," "El Mudo," and "La Cañada del Principio."
And, finally, the last story of the collection, "No se asombre, sar-

gento," in a category of its own, participates in both realities described in the other seven stories of the collection.

The first story of the collection, and the one from which the collection takes its name, is "Benzulul." It is the story of Juan Rodríguez Benzulul, an Indian who feels himself defeated and condemned to wander the roads of Tenejapa after death because of his Indian name. He longs to possess the name of Encarnación Salvatierra, because he knows that then he could be like Encarnación, free in life to act and in death to rest, for an Indian name implies impotence and eternal unrest, while a Spanish name signifies power and eternal peace. "Los muertos sin nombre ya no guardan la semilla, dice la nana Porfiria, pero tienen que llevar hojas pa envolverla. Se les cae la semilla cuando mueren, pero tienen la obligación de buscarla. En la noche con luna es cuando buscan las hojas. . . . Los que tienen nombre se quedan con la semilla en su lugar. Cuando yo muera voy a seguir caminando este camino: Juan Rodríguez Benzulul no dejará el camino. ¡Si consigo un nombre todo cambia! Encarnación Salvatierra va a morir sabroso. No va a aparecer en la noche. No va a espantar. No va a llorar. Tiene nombre" [88:21].

Therefore, when "la nana Porfiria" gives him Encarnación's name, Benzulul goes through the town a changed man, and he acquires a strength previously unknown to him. But Encarnación Salvatierra soon tires of Benzulul's attempt to take his name, and to prevent him from continuing in his attempt, he hangs him from a tree and cuts out his tongue.

There are many aspects to this story pertinent to our discussion of the cult of death. The first sentence of "Benzulul" establishes a relationship between man and nature which is evident throughout the entire collection. "Mientras avazanba por la vereda, una parte de su cuerpo se iba quedando en las marcas de sus huellas" [88:13]. The distinction between man and nature is blurred; the two mutually influence each other and are complementary parts of a greater whole, a cosmic process in which nothing is ever lost, but merely changed in form. Benzulul expresses this idea by means of the following metaphor: "Cuando hay un ocurrido, [el río] lo convierte en piedrita redonda y se lo guarda en el fondo. . . . Las piedritas tán siempre guardadas y allí van creciendo. Son huevos de montaña. Cuando es el tiempo acabalado, se hacen piedrotas pa lavar ropa o pa jimbarse de cabeza al río. Después crecen más y se van a donde falte un cerro" [88:15].

The distinction between life and death is also blurred. They, too, mutually influence one another and are seen as complementary parts of a cosmic process. Benzulul's world is peopled with both the living and the dead. The nameless dead wander the roads in search of "hojas para envolver la semilla" and are especially visible by moonlight or to dogs.

> Cuando hay luna las cosas cambian. . . . Asoman cosas del fondo de los ríos. . . . También asoman muertos. Muertos que, como el Martín, como mi tata y mi nana, que, como yo, no tuvieron nombre. Lo andan buscando pa cubrir la semilla. A mí no me gusta encontrar espantos. Pero la luna los trae al camino y el camino es de todos. . . .
> Los perros miran a los muertos.   [88:18]

The constant repetition of words or sentences which serve as a kind of *estribillo* in "Benzulul," and throughout the collection, gives to these stories and to the lives described therein a circular quality. Man, nature, life, and death are presented as complementary parts of a vast life cycle in which negative and positive labels are out of place. It is, therefore, the cult of death of pre-Conquest Mexico which we see in these stories, uncontaminated by the centuries.

The intimate relationship between man and nature is a concept emphasized in each of the four stories dealing with the indigenous man. In each of these, and especially in "Vientooo" and "Patrocinio Tipá," it is this concept which determines the protagonist's attitude toward life and death. In "Vientooo," for example, Matías allows a snake to bite him, because there is no moon and he has been destined from birth to die by snake bite during a full moon. "Yo, mirálo, solo lo voy a morir cuando lo busque la culebra que lo mamó las chichis de mi nana cuando nací. Noche de luna es que tiene que ser, pa que me haga su efecto; pa que me haga enjundia. ¡De otro modo dónde vas a creer que yo me muera!" [88:65]

Therefore, he speaks to the snake and reaches out to stroke her, saying, "—Ya viniste, hermanita. ¿Por qué me querés llevar? Ahora que no hay luna. Sólo con luna es que me podés llevar. Que me puedo morir. ¿A quí vinistes, hermanita?" [88:77]

Even after the first bite, his faith in his destiny is unaltered.

> —¿Por qué me mordiste, hermanita? Yo te iba a acariciar.
> ¿Pero acaso te olvidaste que a mí no me podés matar? Sólo
> que fuera noche de luna podés fregarme. Y eso, yo queri-
> endo.
> La nauyaca volvió a enroscarse y preparó el cuello nueva-
> mente. Los ojos, pequeños dardos, y la lengua con movi-
> mientos lentos, primero, y muy rápidos después.
> —Mordéme otra . . . pa que veás. Pa que te des cuenta que
> al Matías no lo podés fregar. . . .
> Y acercó la mano, hasta casi rozar la cabeza triangular.
> Uno, dos, tres, mordidas rápidas.   [88:78]

And still, when the pain becomes severe, he refuses to take
the antidote. "¿Pa qué? Si yo no puedo morir en noche oscura"
[88:79]. In his agony, he notices that the south wind for which he
has prayed for days comes to sweep away the rain and clouds and
to reveal behind the clouds the full moon which brings with it his
death.

"El Caguamo" pertains to the second category of stories in
Benzulul. It is the story of a chain of death passed on from father
to son and strengthened by a town, a people, and a way of life dedicated to the cult of violence, a product of the cult of death. Primitivo Barragán, El Caguamo, was a good man, respected, and a hard
worker. And yet his father, though not a bad man, had died by the
gun, and his last act had been to blow open the head of his assassin
with the gun which later passed as an inheritance to his son.

Primitivo has no desire to live by violence. He merely wants
to make a secure, peaceful life with his woman, Eugenia. But the
town makes that impossible. They begin vicious gossip which
forces Eugenia's father to seek to avenge his soiled honor. But his
attempt to ambush and kill Primitivo fails, and instead Primitivo
is forced, in self-defense, to kill his father-in-law with the gun he
has inherited from his father. More killings follow, all unneces-
sary and unwanted by Primitivo. His wife can no longer bear his
presence. His only hope lies in his unborn son. But Eugenia, to
avenge her father, aborts herself, and Primitivo, in an act of grief-
produced madness, tears open her stomach, burns his house, kills
his animals, and flees. But he flees not so much to free himself
from reprisals as he does to free himself from the necessity of con-

tinuing to kill. He is afraid that he will not be able to break the chain of death of which he is a link, that "they" will not allow it. " 'No quero volver a hacerlo. Ese sudor pegajoso y la sangre rebotando como piedras; ese susto que da el andar matando no quero volverlo a sentir. Que me dejen quieto. Que me dejen solo y seguiré siendo hombre bueno. Ellos me hicieron creminar y pueden volver a hacerlo,' pensaba el Caguamo viendo hacia Jitotol" [88:55]. And yet, one wonders if among a people so dedicated to the cult of violence and the cult of death a man like El Caguamo can ever really escape.

El Vaquerizo, protagonist of "El Mudo," was also a man of peace. He had avoided any involvement in the Revolution which raged around him, and yet he was now facing a firing squad, because, struck mute by a fall from his horse, he could not tell the revolutionary forces the location of the guns of the Municipal Council. He did not know their location, but he was unable even to tell them that. And no one believed that he was truly unable to speak. So he died before the firing squad, and they said of him, "Se murió en su línea; en su mero relajo; era macho el Vaquerizo" [88:101].

Reality in this story assumes a nightmarish form. Life and death seem to float in a senseless vacuum. El Vaquerizo notes precisely this situation in the first pages of the story. "Vaquerizo no movió la vista de la puerta. Le parecía que toda esta situación era de a mentiras, de puro vacilón. Eso de que le digan a uno que ya mañana no va a hacer nada más que ir a poner el pecho para que lo venadeen sin oportunidad de que se defiende, como si fuera un coyote matrero, era a lo que no podía acostumbrarse el Vaquerizo" [88:86–87].

This same nightmarish quality is evident in "La Cañada del Principio," but at least in that story there is a logical motive for Neófito's presence in the senseless war arena. He is there to avenge his father's death at the hands of the *federales*. But that is not so with El Vaquerizo.

And yet, faced with death, no matter how absurd, and despite his previous fears and efforts to escape her, El Vaquerizo faces his destiny without fear and without any thought of escape. As Zepeda explains it, "No tenía ya esperanzas; tampoco temor; no le temblaron las piernas como dicen que les pasa a los fusilados, ni le dieron ganas de llorar. No era por valentía. Nunca tuvo fama de eso; era por otra cosa. La muerte estaba allí, de cuerpo entero y para que le daba más vueltas. El llano se abría enfrente de la barda que le servía de paredón; se iba hasta más allá de los sembrados de caña y en el camino había matorrales y piedras donde esconderse. Pero el Vaquerizo no pensó en salir corriendo; en escaparse" [88:96].

A similar situation prevails in the last story and, in my opinion, the best story of the collection, "No se asombre, sargento." The protagonist of this story was afraid when his father died, and yet, because he remembers the words passed on to him as an inheritance by his dying father, the end products of a lifetime of accumulated wisdom, he loses that fear completely at the hour of his own death. "La muerte no mata," his father had told him, "lo que mata es la suerte" [88:161]. "Lo bueno aquí en el campo es saber cuando se va uno a morir; que en el campo la muerte no es más que un sucedido que a juerzas tiene que llegar y casi siempre es hasta una salida pa los problemas" [88:158]. "Acordáte siempre, nunca debes de sentirte solo; onde quiera que estés yo voy a andar contigo" [88:161].

Fathers are instruments of continuity for their sons in Zepeda's stories. From his father, Primitivo Barragán had inherited his ability as a marksman and his fate as a killer. The protagonist of "No se asombre, sargento," from his father, has learned to die.

> Ansina jué como se murió mi tata. Ansina me enseñó a morir. Ansina jué que me dijo lo que se debe hacer. . . . sé que el tata tenía razón cuando me dijo que la muerte no viene a ser más que un caballo matrero al que algún día tenemos que montar. Por eso es que estoy tranquilo señor. Y usté, sargento, también debe de estar igual. Hoy le toca tirar a usté, mañana le tocará recibir.
>
> ¡Bueno! yo ya acabé de hacer la tumba. No más le recomiendo que me entierren hasta el fondo. Usté dice, sargento, en dónde me pongo pa que me fusile.   [88:163–64]

Confronted by imminent death, the protagonist of "No se asombre, sargento" discusses with spontaneous familiarity the phenomenon and the counsel given him by his dying father. As Enrique Congrains Martin points out, "La muerte como una experiencia natural, normal, 'como un sucedido que a juerzas tiene que llegar,' es la idea que sostiene el protagonista, encarnando una actitud vital muy arraigada en el campesinado mexicano" [87:212].

Man faced with death is a theme which appears in all of the stories of *Benzulul*. It is the last story of the collection, though, which best expresses the attitude toward death which prevails throughout the work.

5

Literary Influences Today:
New Trends in Mexican Literature

I T HAS BEEN ESTABLISHED that the bases of the Mexican
cult of death lie in the indigenous Mexican culture and
in pre-Conquest Spanish culture and that the fusion of these two
cultures created the somewhat extreme social phenomenon which
we have indicated as being very much alive and evident in Mexico today. In regard to the fusion of cultures, though, there is one
significant feature which must be pointed out. Clara Passafari de
Gutiérrez, in discussing the works of Juan Rulfo, has stated that
"Rulfo no presenta la vida de México sino el alma mexicana en
lo más hondo de su atavismo" [70:75]. The cult of death is an outstanding element of that soul, and in almost all of the stories discussed herein, we find that it appears to be a phenomenon which
reverts not to an earlier Catholic prototype, but to early indigenous culture. Thus, R. A. M. VanZantwijk tells us that "the introduction of Christianity into Mexico was the logical consequence
of the Aztec view of life. Christianity is thus, as far as confessed
by Indians, taken in the Aztec religious sense and as such has
never been, and never will be, able to free itself from their beliefs"
[7:114]. The Aztec attitude toward death, then, was refined and
augmented by the Christian counterpart, but the phenomenon
which one sees reflected in most of the stories herein, though it
owes its survival and development to the fusion of Christian and
indigenous attitudes, in reality exhibits a far closer kinship to the
latter.

In regard to literature, it has been illustrated that the phenomenon was an outstanding element of ancient, indigenous Mexican literature and of pre-Conquest Spanish literature, and that it
is also a strong element in the contemporary short story of the
period 1947–60. The six authors discussed herein represent the
major regions of Mexico and thereby illustrate that the cult of

death is by no means a purely regional phenomenon, but is one which manifests itself in the work of writers from all regions of the country.

The study of manifestations of the cult of death in the short stories of each of these six authors substantiates the hypothesis that the cult of death is a significant, perhaps the most significant, element of the modern Mexican psyche and that as such it logically manifests itself in all genres of contemporary Mexican literature. That this volume deals with only one of these by no means implies that the findings herein are not equally applicable to the novel, to poetry, or to other genres.

It is still difficult to evaluate accurately the degree to which manifestations of the cult of death have been a significant feature of the Mexican short story since 1960. This is due primarily to the lack of critical material dealing with the works of the younger artists and, even more important, to the inaccessibility of their works, which tend to be dispersed haphazardly throughout the myriad journals, magazines, and newspapers of Mexico, many of which are regional publications with no international, and sometimes not even national, circulation. My own readings, though, have led me to certain tentative conclusions concerning recent thematic trends significant to our discussion of manifestations of the cult of death.

There seems to be a tendency among younger writers to move away from a conscientious attempt to express "the Mexican" toward an expression of more universal themes. Cosmopolitan settings and mentalities are being explored where, during the fifties, the concern was more for the rural. It is as if earlier writers had discovered and revealed the nature and source of the Mexican character and younger writers are turning now to more universal themes in an attempt to extend themselves beyond the limits of their nationality. For example, young writers such as Gustavo Sáinz and José Agustín have, for the first time in Mexico, attempted to reveal in literature the world of the adolescent. And the human problems dealt with in the more recent short stories are of a more complex nature than those basic problems of survival, life, and death dealt with in earlier works. Social problems are also of a more complex nature than those formerly dealt with, which tended to be rural problems such as the Indian and agrarian reform.

The younger writers are a more self-searching group. They are concerned less with revealing their nature as Mexicans than with revealing their nature as individuals in the more universal sense, and in their writing they appear to be conscientiously seeking a *sui generis* form. There is an evident bitter humor and cynicism in many of their works and, especially significant, a snobbism which was completely lacking in the literature of most of the writers of the fifties who have been discussed herein.

Generally speaking, then, one might say that, due to the more subjective and universal nature of the new Mexican short story, manifestations of the cult of death are a less prominent element of the genre today than they were previously, or at least they are present in a far more subtle form.

This is not to say that there do not exist young writers who are following in the tradition of established artists such as Juan Rulfo, José Revueltas, or Rosario Castellanos, for there are many. An outstanding example among these is Tomás Mojarro, who has been called an "heredero directo" of Rulfo, Yáñez, and Revueltas [70:214]. Nevertheless, one must take into account the ascendency of a new group of writers whose concerns are more cosmopolitan, more universal, and in whose writings manifestations of the cult of death are less prevalent. Only time and future critical evaluation will tell to what extent this tendency will prevail in Mexican literature.

We must not forget, though, that as a social phenomenon the cult of death is still of supreme significance in Mexico. It therefore seems most likely that as we examine in further retrospect the short story production of the last twelve years, we will find that, despite new tendencies, manifestations of the cult of death will abound.

References

1. Soustelle, Jacques. *The Daily Life of the Aztecs on the Eve of the Spanish Conquest.* Translated by Patrick O'Brian. New York, 1962.
2. Sahagún, Bernardino de. *Historia general de las cosas de Nueva España.* Edited by A. M. Garibay. 4 vols. Mexico, 1969.
3. León-Portilla, Miguel. *Pre-Columbian Literatures of Mexico.* Translated by Grace Lobanov and Miguel León-Portilla. Norman, Okla., 1969.
4. Fernández, Justino. *Mexican Art.* Verona, Italy, 1965.
5. Séjourné, Laurette. *Burning Water: Thought and Religion in Ancient Mexico.* New York, 1956.
6. Nicholson, Irene. *Mexican and Central American Mythology.* Verona, Italy, 1967.
7. VanZantwijk, R. A. M. "Aztec Hymns As the Expression of the Mexican Philosophy of Life." *Internationales Archiv für Ethnographie* 48:67–118.
8. Séjourné, Laurette. "Los sacrificios humanos: Religiosos o políticos?" *Cuadernos americanos* 17:127–49.
9. VonHagen, Victor. *The Aztec: Man and Tribe.* New York, 1962.
10. Garibay, Angel María. *Historia de la literatura nahuatl.* 2 vols. Mexico, 1953.
11. Hvidtfeldt, Arild. *Teotl and Ixiptlatli: Some Central Conceptions in Ancient Mexican Religion with a General Introduction on Cult and Myth.* Copenhagen, 1958.
12. Arias-Larreta, Abraham. *Literaturas aborígenes: Azteca, Incaica, Maya-Quiche.* Los Angeles, 1951.
13. Arias-Larreta, Abraham. *Pre-Columbian Literatures.* Los Angeles, 1964.
14. León-Portilla, Miguel. *Aztec Thought and Culture: A Study of the Ancient Nahuatl Mind.* Translated by Jack Emory Davis. Norman, Okla., 1963.
15. Ellis, Havelock. *The Soul of Spain.* Cambridge, England, 1931.
16. Vélez, Joseph F. "El tema de la muerte en la novela contemporánea mexicana." Ph.D. Dissertation, University of Oklahoma, 1969.
17. Unamuno, Miguel de. *Essays and Soliloquies.* New York, 1925.
18. Ilie, Paul. *Unamuno: An Existential View of Self and Society.* Madison, Wis., 1967.
19. Unamuno, Miguel de. *Our Lord Don Quixote: The Life of Don Quixote and Sancho with Related Essays,* translated by Anthony Kerrigan. In *Selected Works of Miguel de Unamuno,* vol. 3, edited by Anthony Kerrigan. Princeton, N. J., 1967.
20. del Río, Angel. *Historia de la literatura española.* 2 vols. New York, 1963.
21. Castro, Américo. *La realidad histórica de España.* Mexico, 1958.
22. Pritchett, V. S. *The Spanish Temper.* New York, 1954.
23. Ayuso Rivera, Juan. *El concepto de la muerte en la poesía romántica española.* Madrid, 1959.

24. Austen, John. *The Story of Don Juan: A Study of the Legend and the Hero.* London, 1939.
25. Huizinga, J. *The Waning of the Middle Ages.* New York, 1924.
26. Ruiz, Juan. *El libro de buen amor.* Edited by Raymond S. Willis. Princeton, 1972.
27. León-Portilla, Miguel. *Los antiguos mexicanos a través de sus crónicas y cantares.* Mexico, 1961.
28. Barnstone, Willis, ed. *Spanish Poetry: From Its Beginnings Through the Nineteenth Century.* New York, 1970.
29. López de Ayala, Pero. *Poesías del Canciller Pero López de Ayala.* 2 vols. New York, 1920.
30. Azáceta, José María, ed. *Cancionero de Juan Alfonso de Baena.* 3 vols. Madrid, 1966.
31. Krause, Anna. *Jorge Manrique and the Cult of Death in the Cuatrocientos.* Publications of the University of California at Los Angeles in Languages and Literatures, vol. 1, no. 3. Berkeley, 1937.
32. Azáceta, José María, ed. *Cancionero de Juan Fernández de Ixar.* Madrid, 1956.
33. Salinas, Pedro. *Ensayos de literatura hispánica: Del "Cantar de mio Cid" a García Lorca.* Madrid, 1961.
34. Romanell, Patrick. *Making of the Mexican Mind.* Freeport, N. Y., 1952.
35. Paz, Octavio. *El laberinto de la soledad.* Mexico, 1965.
36. Nunez, Theron A. "Mexican Attitudes Toward Death." Paper delivered at the Annual Meeting of the American Academy of Psychotherapists, Washington, D. C., 1964.
37. Ewing, Russell C., ed. *Six Faces of Mexico.* Tucson, Ariz., 1966.
38. Hewes, Gordon W. "Mexicans in Search of the 'Mexican': Notes on Mexican National Character Studies." *American Journal of Economics and Sociology* 13:209–23.
39. Díaz Guerrero, Rogelio. *Estudios de psicología del mexicano.* Mexico, 1961.
40. Gómez Robleda, José. *Psicología del mexicano.* Mexico, 1965.
41. Caso, Alfonso. *El pueblo del sol.* Mexico, 1953.
42. Marks, John. *To the Bullfights Again.* New York, 1967.
43. Tavera A., Xavier. "El mexicano." *Hispanoamericana* 1:4–18.
44. Jiménez, A. *Picardía mexicana.* Mexico, 1961.
45. Price, W. J. "Birth, Childhood, and Death in Todos Santos." *Practical Anthropology* 13(2):85–99.
46. Garrett, W. E. "South to Mexico City." *National Geographic* 134(2):145–93.
47. Castaneda, Carlos. *A Separate Reality: Further Conversations with Don Juan.* New York, 1971.
48. Castaneda, Carlos. *Journey to Ixtlan: The Lessons of Don Juan.* New York, 1972.
49. Nazoa, Aguiles. *Cuentos contemporáneos hispanoamericanos.* La Paz, Bolivia, 1957.
50. Aguilera-Malta, Demetrio. "Charla con Seymour Menton: El cuento hispanoamericano." *Mundo nuevo* 56:49–52.
51. Harss, Luis, and Barbara Dohmann. *Into the Mainstream: Conversations with Latin American Writers.* New York, 1969.
52. Benítez, Antonio. "Prólogo." In *El llano en llamas/Pedro Páramo,* by Juan Rulfo. Havana, 1968.
53. Gómez Gleason, María Teresa. "Juan Rulfo y el mundo de su próxima novela *La cordillera.*" *Siempre* 679 (29 June 1966):63–65.
54. Eastman, Richard M. *A Guide to the Novel.* San Francisco, 1965.
55. Rulfo, Juan. *El llano en llamas.* 7th ed. Mexico, 1965.

56. Rodríguez Alcalá, Hugo. *El arte de Juan Rulfo*. Mexico, 1965.
57. Xirau, Ramón. "Juan Rulfo, nuevo escritor de México." *Insula* 16(179):4.
58. Irby, James. *La influencia de William Faulkner en cuatro narradores hispano-americanos*. Mexico, 1956.
59. Estrada, Ricardo. "Los indicios de *Pedro Páramo*." *Revista de la Universidad de San Marcos* 65:13.
60. Carballo, Emmanuel. *El cuento mexicano en el siglo XX*. Mexico, 1964.
61. Wellek, René, and Austin Warren. *Theory of Literature*. New York, 1956.
62. Chávarri, Raúl. "Una novela en la frontera de la vida y la muerte." *Cuadernos hispanoamericanos* 66:174–79.
63. Hill, Diane E. "Integración, desintegración e intensificación en los cuentos de Juan Rulfo." *Revista iberoamericana* 34:331–38.
64. de la Colina, José. "Notas sobre Juan Rulfo." *Siempre* 26:133–38.
65. Couffon, Claude. "El arte de Juan Rulfo." *Siempre* 714:43–51.
66. Schade, George D., trans. "Introduction to Juan Rulfo." In *The Burning Plain*, by Juan Rulfo. Austin, Tex., 1967.
67. León de Garay, Alfonso. *Una aproximación a la psicología del mexicano*. Mexico, 1958.
68. Torres-Ríoseco, Arturo. *Aspects of Spanish American Literature*. Seattle, Wash., 1963.
69. Arenas, Reinaldo. "El páramo en llamas." *El mundo*, 7 July 1968, pp. 113–28.
70. Passafari de Gutiérrez, Clara. *Los cambios en la concepción y estructura de la narrativa mexicana desde 1947*. Santa Fe, Argentina, 1968.
71. Revueltas, José. *Dormir en tierra*. Xalapa, Mexico, 1960.
72. Valadés, Edmundo. "El cuento mexicano reciente." *Armas y letras* 3(4):19–39.
73. Chumacero, Alí. "José Revueltas." *Letras de México* 4:5.
74. Castellanos, Rosario. *Ciudad Real*. Xalapa, Mexico, 1960.
75. Cervera, Juan. "Conversación con Juan Rulfo" and "El gallo ilustrado." *El día*, 16 June 1968, p. 3.
76. Donoso Pareja, Miguel. "Algunas consideraciones sobre la joven narrativa mexicana." *El día*, 5 August 1969, p. 12.
77. Reeve, Richard M. "Annotated Bibliography on Carlos Fuentes." *Hispania* 53:597–652.
78. Salazar Mallén, Rubén. "Bombones por el snobismo." *Mañana* 22(11,119):38.
79. Paz, Octavio. "La máscara y la transparencia." "La cultura en México." *Siempre* 726:iv–v.
80. Fuentes, Carlos. "Chac Mool." In *Seis cuentos latinoamericanos*. Montevideo, 1969.
81. Carballo, Emmanuel. "Los días enmascarados." *Revista de la Universidad de México* 9,7:4,16.
82. Carballo, Emmanuel. *Cuentistas mexicanos modernos*. 2 vols. Mexico, 1956.
83. Rodríguez Monegal, Emir. "El mundo mágico de Carlos Fuentes." *Número* (Montevideo) 1,2:144–59.
84. Espejo y Díaz, Beatriz. "Carlos Fuentes: Los días enmascarados." *Filosofía y letras* 55–56:261–73.
85. Dueñas, Guadalupe. "Autopresentación." *Abside* 30(3):357–65.
86. Dueñas, Guadalupe. *Tiene la noche un árbol*. Mexico, 1958.
87. Congrains Martin, Enrique, ed. *Antología contemporánea del cuento mexicano*. Mexico, 1963.
88. Zepeda, Eraclio. *Benzulul*. Xalapa, Mexico, 1959.
89. Azuela, Mariano. *Los de abajo*. Edited by John E. Englekirk and Lawrence B. Kiddle. New York, 1945.

UNIVERSITY OF FLORIDA MONOGRAPHS

Humanities

No. 1: *Uncollected Letters of James Gates Percival,* edited by Harry R. Warfel

No. 2: *Leigh Hunt's Autobiography: The Earliest Sketches,* edited by Stephen F. Fogle

No. 3: *Pause Patterns in Elizabethan and Jacobean Drama,* by Ants Oras

No. 4: *Rhetoric and American Poetry of the Early National Period,* by Gordon E. Bigelow

No. 5: *The Background of* The Princess Casamassima, by W. H. Tilley

No. 6: *Indian Sculpture in the John and Mable Ringling Museum of Art,* by Roy C. Craven, Jr.

No. 7: *The Cestus. A Mask,* edited by Thomas B. Stroup

No. 8: Tamburlaine, Part I, *and Its Audience,* by Frank B. Fieler

No. 9: *The Case of John Darrell: Minister and Exorcist,* by Corinne Holt Rickert

No. 10: *Reflections of the Civil War in Southern Humor,* by Wade H. Hall

No. 11: *Charles Dodgson, Semeiotician,* by Daniel F. Kirk

No. 12: *Three Middle English Religious Poems,* edited by R. H. Bowers

No. 13: *The Existentialism of Miguel de Unamuno,* by José Huertas-Jourda

No. 14: *Four Spiritual Crises in Mid-Century American Fiction,* by Robert Detweiler

No. 15: *Style and Society in German Literary Expressionism,* by Egbert Krispyn

No. 16: *The Reach of Art: A Study in the Prosody of Pope,* by Jacob H. Adler

No. 17: *Malraux, Sartre, and Aragon as Political Novelists,* by Catharine Savage

No. 18: *Las Guerras Carlistas y el Reinado Isabelino en la Obra de Ramón del Valle-Inclán,* por María Dolores Lado

No. 19: *Diderot's* Vie de Sénèque: A *Swan Song Revised,* by Douglas A. Bonneville

No. 20: *Blank Verse and Chronology in Milton,* by Ants Oras

No. 21: *Milton's Elisions,* by Robert O. Evans

No. 22: *Prayer in Sixteenth-Century England,* by Faye L. Kelly

No. 23: *The Strangers: The Tragic World of Tristan L'Hermite,* by Claude K. Abraham

No. 24: *Dramatic Uses of Biblical Allusion in Marlowe and Shakespeare,* by James H. Sims

No. 25: *Doubt and Dogma in Maria Edgeworth,* by Mark D. Hawthorne

No. 26: *The Masses of Francesco Soriano,* by S. Philip Kniseley

No. 27: *Love as Death in* The Iceman Cometh, by Winifred Dusenbury Frazer

No. 28: *Melville and Authority,* by Nicholas Canaday, Jr.

No. 29: *Don Quixote: Hero or Fool? A Study in Narrative Technique,* by John J. Allen

No. 30: *Ideal and Reality in the Fictional Narratives of Théophile Gautier,* by Albert B. Smith

No. 31: *Negritude as a Theme in the Poetry of the Portuguese-Speaking World,* by Richard A. Preto-Rodas

No. 32: *The Criticism of Photography as Art: The Photographs of Jerry Uelsmann,* by John L. Ward

No. 33: *The Kingdom of God in the Synoptic Tradition,* by Richard H. Hiers

No. 34: *Dante Gabriel Rossetti's Versecraft,* by Joseph F. Vogel

No. 35: *T. S. Eliot's Concept of Language: A Study of Its Development,* by Harry T. Antrim

No. 36: *The Consolatio Genre in Medieval English Literature,* by Michael H. Means

No. 37: *Melville's Angles of Vision,* by A. Carl Bredahl, Jr.

No. 38: *The Historical Jesus and the Kingdom of God,* by Richard H. Hiers

No. 39: *In Adam's Garden: A Study of John Clare's Pre-Asylum Poetry,* by Janet M. Todd

No. 40: *Democracy, Stoicism, and Education: An Essay in the History of Freedom and Reason,* by Robert R. Sherman

No. 41: *On Defining the Proper Name,* by John Algeo

No. 42: *The Henley-Stevenson Quarrel,* by Edward H. Cohen

No. 43: *E.G. and E.G.O.: Emma Goldman and* The Iceman Cometh, by Winifred L. Frazer

No. 44: *The Mexican Cult of Death in Myth and Literature,* by Barbara L. C. Brodman